Judy Garland

Beyond the Rainbow

Judy Garland
Beyond the Rainbow

SHERIDAN MORLEY AND RUTH LEON

ARCADE PUBLISHING • NEW YORK

For Ann and Barry Mishon,
who love Judy as much as we do.

SM & RL

First U.S. Edition

ISBN 1-55970-491-8
Library of Congress Catalog Card Number 99-72549
Library of Congress Cataloging-in-Publication information is available.

Published in United States by Arcade Publishing, Inc., New York
Distributed by Time Warner Trade Publishing

2 4 6 8 10 9 7 5 3 1

Printed in Spain

FRONTISPIECE Judy at the moment when MGM were at last willing to let
her grow up – how could they ignore the girl next door any longer?

Contents

Introduction

She was born Frances Ethel Gumm in Grand Rapids, Minnesota, on 10 June 1922. She died Judy Garland of a drugs overdose in London on 22 June 1969, just twelve days after her forty-seventh birthday. Since then, countless writers on both sides of the Atlantic have told her story in terms of the doomed child star who crossed over the rainbow and somehow never came back. But now, for the first time, exactly thirty years after her untimely death, it can surely be seen that the story of Judy Garland is not just a tale of chemical abuse, or too many disastrous marriages, or even a chronic lack of professional or private self-discipline, but a story of how the ruthless studio system mistreated one of the greatest screen stars.

We are writing here of a woman whose Palace Theater concerts in the New York of the early 1950s set attendance records that have to this day never been broken. We are also writing of a woman who between 1936 and 1963 made thirty-four films, at least two a year, among them such all-time classics as *The Wizard of Oz* and *Babes In Arms*, both in 1939, *For Me and My Gal* (1942), *Meet Me in St Louis* (1944), *Easter Parade* (1948) and *A Star is Born* (1954).

Because Judy Garland drew tears for her life as well as her performances, it is all too easy to confuse the two. To underrate her screen talent, however, is to overlook the main reason why we still care about her essentially tragic life.

RIGHT *Before her luck ran out – a studio portrait for a film that never got made.* ☆

Judy danced with Mickey Rooney, Fred Astaire, Ray Bolger, Gene Kelly and Cyd Charisse. Twice nominated for an Oscar, she won a rare special miniature Academy Award for *The Wizard of Oz*, and we have not yet begun to consider her hundreds of radio and television appearances, nor the albums of her hits which continue to be re-released at the rate of at least half a dozen a year.

Like Marilyn Monroe, her destiny was to have a life often more dramatic than her work, and like Elizabeth Taylor, her hospital stays often required more time than her movies. Throughout her life, headaches, sore throats, earaches, insomnia, fatigue and countless other illnesses plagued her, and yet morning after morning she would turn up for studio work only an hour or two after closing an informal nightclub act.

With the posthumous wisdom of thirty years of psychiatric exploration, it must now be clear that she was the victim of highs and lows most usually associated with manic depression, but at the time the studio solution was simply to fill her with so many pills that friends said most mornings she actually rattled.

As we write, at the beginning of 1999, Judy is thirty years dead and *The Wizard of Oz* is sixty years alive. If she is to live for ever, it will be almost entirely because of her journey to the Emerald City. As the movie historian David Thomson wrote of this anniversary, '*The Wizard of Oz* is sepia bursting into Technicolor, Kansas in

a dream fever, figures of real life inflated in fantasy, flying monkeys, Frank Morgan as the Wizard himself, Margaret Hamilton as the Wicked Witch of the West ("What a world!"), the splendiferous Bert Lahr, the wistful Ray Bolger, the frankly dull Jack Haley (someone had to be dull), the Munchkins and, of course, Judy. How does it all work? The answer is ruby slippers.'

But the real story of Judy Garland is of someone who lived and loved and died entirely in the public eye. In that sense she was the first victim of the collapse of the Hollywood studio system which, until her time, protected its top box-office stars behind a wall of discreet and uncommunicative publicists. Judy was the first one they left hanging out to dry.

The 'what' of Judy Garland's life is well known. The 'how' and the 'why' are what this book is all about.

1. *Little Miss Gumm*

1922—1932

It was her fifth husband, Mickey Deans, who found her. Early on the morning of 22 June 1969, looking for her to take a phone call from Los Angeles, Deans discovered the bathroom door of their borrowed London house locked. Climbing in through a window, he found Judy dead. Some hours later, the Chelsea coroner, Gavin Thurston, reported that Judy Garland had died from 'an incautious self-overdosage of sleeping pills'. He added, 'Miss Garland had taken, perhaps in a state of confusion from previous doses, more barbiturates than her body could tolerate.'

> '*My mother was truly a stage mother, a mean one. She would stand in the wings, and if I didn't feel good she'd say: "You go out there and sing or I'll wrap you round the bedpost and break you off short!"*'

At forty-seven, only a few days after the collapse of yet one more disastrous concert tour, Judy, alone in the bathroom of yet another home that was not her own, had reached the end of the Yellow Brick Road, a route which had started in the American Midwest early in the 1920s, had led to California in its heyday, and to a career still unrivalled in the whole history of Hollywood.

Like Marilyn Monroe before her, Judy lived a short, sharp life. Her untimely death has ensured for her, over three decades, the kind of martyrdom granted to only a very few, and it is arguable that, had she lived, her already collapsed career would have done her considerably more damage in the public eye than did her early death.

To understand the end of her life, we have to go back to its very beginning.

If not exactly born in a trunk, the one she was to sing about in *A Star is Born*, Judy was at least (on 10 June 1922, in Grand Rapids, Minnesota) born into a show-business family. Her father, Frank Avent Gumm, was then the manager of the local New Theater. He and his wife, Ethel Marian Milne, had started out as a vaudeville team, and Judy's only siblings, Virginia (two years older) and Mary-Jane (seven years older), were already preparing to sing duets on their father's stage to the accompaniment of their mother's piano.

Their parents had actually been hoping so fervently that Judy would be a boy that her original birth announcement is spelt Francis instead of Frances; but when they recovered from this disappointment (a psychiatrist could argue that it was Judy's first rejection), little Baby Gumm became the family mascot. When she was two and a half, during the Christmas season of 1924, Judy escaped backstage and, to her parents' horror, was soon to be found centre-stage in the spotlight. 'It was,' she recalled, 'Amateur Night at my father's theatre and I was desperate to join in … even then I was a very determined little girl. I ran onstage and sang "Jingle Bells" over and over again, with Mother scowling at me from the piano until Father had to march out on to the stage and carry me off.'

By the time she was five, Judy had developed an allergy so severe that she had an almost constant fever, and the family decided that a move to the drier, hotter temperatures of Lancaster, California, might prove helpful. There were also other reasons, as Judy's mother later recalled: 'If you must know, we wanted to get away from the coal bills and the storm windows. The whole thing started with my husband saying, "Let's try California for a week" and what we really loved there was the climate, roses and balmy skies in the middle of winter. This was the place, we decided, this is it.'

Before they left Grand Rapids, however, little Baby Gumm was to be found with her sisters performing such blackface routines as 'The Kinky Kids Parade' on her father's stage and any others they could commandeer. And if vaudeville bookings were few and far between, there was still the annual

BELOW *Judy's parents, Frank and Ethel Gumm, at the start of their tortured marriage.* ☆

RIGHT *The Gumm Sisters go to work.* ☆

local Dry Goods company trade fair. 'A hatbox,' as the local paper reported, 'slightly larger than usual, was carried on to the stage. In a few moments it became active: the lid opened as if by magic and out came the little three-year old Frances Ethel Gumm, who looked cautiously around before finally crawling out of the box and giving a lively performance of the Charleston. This was the undoubted hit of the whole trade show, and a round of applause greeted the little dancer as she went through her antics like a seasoned Follies girl.'

Frank, a heavy drinker, had by this time given up the management of the Grand Rapids theatre, and the entire Gumm clan was now in on the act. Frank and Ethel sang highlights from the classics and their three little girls provided some livelier interludes. On a series of tacky vaudeville tours, however, it soon became painfully clear that while audiences across the country had very little time or enthusiasm for the parents, they were willing to be won over by the all-singing, all-dancing Gumm sisters.

Ethel, always the brains of the family (insofar as there were any), realized as soon as they got to California, firstly that movies would soon kill live entertainment, and secondly that, for the moment at least, sister acts were still a draw. Frank bought the local theatre in downtown Lancaster and began showing movies, in the intervals of which his girls and his wife provided live entertainment. It didn't take long for the Gumm Sisters to make their vaudeville debut on the road, even if they were

FRANK AND ETHEL GUMM

unfortunately billed last, under Added Attractions, and misspelt as The Glumm Sisters. This was at the Oriental Theater of the Chicago World's Fair of 1934, when Judy was twelve. Top of the bill was the comic George Jessel who, realizing not only that Gumm could so easily become Glumm (not to mention rhyme with dumb, crumb and bum), always took the credit for having dreamed up a new name for little Frances Gumm.

Years later, on an Ed Sullivan show, Jessel noted gracefully that even if he had named her Hiawatha Titanic, the child's talent was such that she would still, inevitably, have become a star. 'Garland' simply came from a local drama critic called Robert Garland who happened to be in Jessel's dressing room when he was thinking about the need for a change of name. As for 'Judy', that came from one of her mother's favourite Hoagy Carmichael songs.

By 1931, the vaudeville circuit was beginning to collapse, along with Frank's health, and the family spent more and more time in their new California home. The marriage between Judy's parents had never been altogether easy. Frank had been gay when they married, and was to return to a bisexual life as soon as the family moved to California. A psychiatrist might want to consider that fact in connection with the strong affiliation in later years between Judy (and, indeed *her* daughter, Liza) and gay audiences the world over. At the time, though, it was the family strife that she remembered, 'As I recall,' said Judy, years later, 'my parents were

separating and getting back together all the time. It was very hard for me to understand what was going on, and I remember clearly the fear I had of those separations.'

Frank moved into a one-room shack near the railroad tracks in Lancaster – though, ever the eccentric, he could have afforded somewhere rather better – while his wife and children moved to a little house on Ivanhoe Drive in the Silver Lake area of Los Angeles, using the money that the girls were now making on occasional radio and vaudeville bookings to pay the rent.

The Gumm Sisters were now all being billed as The Garland Sisters, but their act was no more successful, although in 1929 they had made a very early 'talkie' short film, sponsored by their Los Angeles stage school, and entitled *Ethel Meglin's Famous Hollywood Wonder Kids*. In this, her very first movie appearance, the seven-year old baby of the troupe can be seen on the far left of the screen wearing a polka-dotted top hat and already almost manically determined to steal the spotlight. As *Variety* noted, 'Baby is the selling end of this so-so trio of sisters.'

George Jessel and, predictably, Mother Gumm realized the problem before anyone else – it was Judy alone who had the talent. On a bill in Detroit, the nearest they ever got to Broadway, the billing for Judy ('Little Girl with the Great Big Voice') began to separate her from her sisters; their mother, by now barely on speaking terms with their ailing, alcoholic father, was only too thrilled to see his name banished for ever.

This was also the year that Judy got her second review, again from *Variety* and again merely confirming what was already common gossip backstage: 'The youngest of the Garlands handles her ballads like a veteran, and gets every note and word over with a personality that hits the audience. Her sisters merely form the background.'

Soon they weren't even to do that. The act technically broke up when Mary-Jane went off to get married in 1935 and Judy, by now fervently managed by her mother (who was fast becoming all too like the stage mother from hell in *Gypsy*), went solo with a cabaret act at a dining, dancing and gambling establishment in Lake Tahoe where the local press were already describing her as 'poignant and unforgettable.'

By a stroke of luck, among the Tahoe tables one night was the songwriter Lew Brown of DeSylva, Brown & Henderson, who fell into conversation with Judy's mother. They soon agreed that vaudeville was effectively dead, and Brown suggested that the time was now ripe for Judy to try getting into films. Back in Lancaster, her father, whom she had always loved best, despite his

many faults, was now gravely ill of spinal meningitis and, ironically, it was in the last few days of his life that Judy 's career began to take off. She got some guest appearances on a highly rated Al Jolson radio show, a Sunday afternoon cabaret engagement at a downtown Los Angeles hotel and, most important of all, the chance to audition for Louis B. Mayer. With her father's death the need for Judy to make a living, not just for her but also for her mother, now became more urgent than ever. And she was still just thirteen years old.

This was the moment when her professional and private lives started to go in opposite directions; she was never to get them together again. Privately, she was the bereaved daughter of a homosexual, unsuccessful, alcoholic but charismatic and beloved father and of a domineering mother who very soon married the man who Judy later believed had been Ethel's lover for some time. Professionally, she was a precocious and starry child who, before her teens had even started, had already made radio and screen debuts and seen her sisters off the stage forever.

2. Ethel Meglin's Wonder Child Goes to Hollywood

1936 — 1937

The audition at MGM was in itself nothing to get excited about. All three Garland sisters had, over the previous two years, frequently been tested without success by Paramount and RKO, and the only real difference this time was that Judy had by now become a solo act. At MGM the staff pianist and arranger, Roger Edens, who was to play a powerful role in the later careers of both Judy and Liza, played 'Zing Went the Strings of my Heart'. Mayer was at first less than impressed, but in deference to the enthusiasm of Edens and his own personal assistant Ida Koverman, he agreed that they could contract Judy on a short-term basis for $100 a week without even a screen test.

> 'A roly-poly girl with eyes like saucers'
> Hedda Hopper

RIGHT Sunday Afternoon (1936) was the short musical filler that brought Judy and Deanna Durbin together for the first and last time. ☆

True, they hadn't the faintest idea what to do with her. MGM already had Jackie Cooper, Freddie Bartholomew and Deanna Durbin as child stars in the making, and when Judy started at the compulsory MGM schoolhouse, she also came across another of their 'stars of tomorrow', a little boy called Mickey Rooney whom she had first met on a radio talent show a couple of years earlier. At this time in 1935, he had already made his name as Puck in *A Midsummer Night's Dream* and was about to go on to *Little Lord Fauntleroy* and *Captains Courageous*.

For Judy, however, the best they could do in the first few months of her contract (which as a minor had to be approved by the local County Court, strongly advised by her mother) was to lend her out to various radio shows hosted by the likes of Wallace Beery and Rudy Vallee. However, as has been well documented elsewhere, MGM in these mid-1930s was not so much a career as a way of life. With almost historical neatness, Louis B. Mayer could now be cast as Judy's missing father, while the rest of her real family (from whom she was getting increasingly detached) could be replaced by a studio family with such father-figures as Clark Gable, brothers like Mickey Rooney, and mothers like Mayer's personal assistant Ida Koverman.

All she needed now was a film, and the very first of these was a curious little fantasy short called *Sunday Afternoon*, in which Judy represented the world of jazz while her great rival Deanna Durbin stood for the world of opera.

LEFT Pigskin Parade *(1936), the only film Judy was to make away from MGM before the 1950s, was a routine college-football campus musical.* ☆

RIGHT *Jack Haley, Patsy Kelly, Johnny Downs and (far right) Betty Grable, introducing Judy to feature filming in* Pigskin Parade. *'Cute, not too pretty, but a pleasingly fetching personality' (New York Times)* ☆

LEFT *Judy with Deanna Durbin in a break from their minimal studies at MGM's Little Red Schoolroom.* ☆

When *Every Sunday* was released the apparently avuncular Louis B. Mayer took an instant dislike to it, failing to understand why his studio was now, it seemed, contracting two very similar little girls when one might be more than enough. His legendary instruction as he left the screening was, 'Fire the fat one', leaving his executives frantically trying to work out whether he had meant Judy or Deanna, who were almost exactly the same weight. They decided to keep Judy, and Deanna was left to start her star career a few months later at Universal, where she remained gainfully employed for many years. 'I,' recalled Judy, 'was the one with an apple in my hand and a dirty face, while she was already the Princess of Transylvania.'

Although Judy's contract was now, albeit accidentally, more secure, Metro still did not hasten to put her into a full-length movie. Instead, they sent her, chaperoned by her mother, across America on a studio promotional tour of remarkably little purpose. On her return to Hollywood later in 1936,

an offer did finally come through but from a rival studio, 20th Century Fox. They wanted her for a college football comedy called *Pigskin Parade*, produced by Darryl Zanuck, and starring the man who would three years later be her Scarecrow in Oz, Jack Haley.

Mayer was delighted with this arrangement. Not only would he get paid for the loan-out but he could discover, at Fox's expense, whether or not Judy had been a wise investment. As her career turned out, this was the only time in nearly twenty years when she was ever loaned out to another studio.

The *New York Times* noted her arrival in feature films with some enthusiasm: 'Newcomer in the cast is Judy Garland, about twelve or thirteen now, about whom the Californians have been enthusing as a radio find ... She is cute, not too pretty, but a pleasingly fetching personality who certainly knows how to sell a song.' She was on her movie way, and love was about to find not only Andy Hardy but also little Miss Garland.

3. Judy Meets Andy Hardy

1936—1938

Back at MGM, Judy's voice had already brought her to the attention of another MGM newcomer, the composer Cole Porter who decided she would be perfect for his new *Born to Dance*. The studio disagreed, however, and, as a consolation prize, cast her in one of their omnibus musicals, *Broadway Melody of 1938*.

'It's apparent that the girl is no mere flash, but has the skill to develop into a box-office wow'
Variety

RIGHT *Judy and Mickey celebrating the all-American milkshake in* Love Finds Andy Hardy *(1938).* ☆

For this, Roger Edens wrote Judy the song that was at last to put her on the studio map. She had, in fact, first sung 'Dear Mr Gable', a musical fan letter, for Clark's thirty-sixth birthday on 1 February 1937 at a party held, in true MGM period style, for the express purpose of diverting press attention from the fact that Gable had just been hit with a paternity suit. Judy, a chubby fourteen, had been forced by the queasily paternal L.B. Mayer to sit on The King's lap. Fortunately, by the time they got to the film, she mercifully was allowed to make do with a framed photograph.

Touched by this remarkable tribute, Gable now gave Judy a quite remarkable gold charm bracelet which was, in effect, her first biography. The individual charms included the seal of her Grand Rapids birthplace, three little girls to represent the original Gumm Sisters, a packet of chewing gum, the autograph of George Jessel, a replica of the MGM studio gate, a microphone, a contract scroll, and this, the last, a little gold book which opened to reveal a photograph of Gable himself.

As for the film, it was essentially an excuse for a series of random musical numbers. Judy played the daughter of Sophie Tucker, memorably cast as a theatrical landlady, and she also got to dance with Buddy Ebsen, the original casting for the Scarecrow of Oz.

The importance of *Broadway Melody of 1938* was not that it quite yet established Judy as a star, but that it marked the beginning of twelve years in which she would be working almost continuously on the MGM lot. Also, having done the birthday tribute to the studio's biggest star, Garland was now officially a daughter of the MGM family.

Critics, however, were still decidedly cautious about Garland's prospects. Of *Broadway Melody of 1938* the *Hollywood Reporter* noted, 'Hers is a distinctive personality well worth careful promotion; with the right material, she just might be a star.'

Quite what that right material might be was still unclear to Metro. All they now knew was that they had her under contract, and that she was willing to work every hour of the studio day. As if to test her stamina, they now threw her into not one but two simultaneous new pictures. The first of these, *Thoroughbreds Don't Cry*, marked her first screen appearance with Mickey Rooney. The plot again cast Judy as the daughter of yet another of Sophie Tucker's boarding-house managers, and the *New York Times* merely noted that 'Judy Garland is the puppy-love interest who tosses off some scorchy rhythm-singing.'

The other film that she made at the same time was released simultaneously and had gone through a series of titles, notably *The Ugly Duckling*, before they finally settled on *Everybody Sing*. For the first time, at least on some posters, Judy got top billing (over Fanny Brice and Allan Jones), while the supporting cast also included Reginald Gardiner doing some remarkable imitations of wallpaper. The rest of the plot equally defied description,

and what might have been the first great vehicle for Judy finished up as a screwball curiosity gone horribly wrong.

But one advantage of the MGM system at the height of its productivity (roughly three new films were released every month) was that nobody really cared about the notices. By the time the movie opened, Judy had already made at least two others.

Her few hours away from the studio, where she was already being heavily dosed with stimulants to keep up her energy level, were spent in a constant state of warfare with the mother she had not forgiven for her unseemly haste in remarrying so rapidly. To make family matters worse, Judy was by now convinced, and by no means entirely wrongly, that her mother had entered into an unholy alliance with Mayer to make sure that she was kept working at all costs.

This did not just mean fourteen-hour days in front of the camera, following two or three in the make-up room. Under the then standard terms of her contract with Metro, she was obliged to spend most of her non-working days criss-crossing the country, introducing her movies in countless cinemas and often performing live songs from their scores.

As if that weren't enough, she also still had a radio contract to broadcast whenever possible as a singer on innumerable comedy shows, again plugging whatever her current film release happened to be.

It was therefore hardly surprising that Judy, who was still only sixteen, already felt bereft of any

BELOW *Judy and her chorus line singing the* Broadway Melody of 1938. ☆

kind of a home life and more than a little distressed that her supposed private and professional guardians only seemed to want her for what they could get out of her. As Judy herself later noted, 'Mother was the real-life Wicked Witch of the West; she was no good for anything except creating chaos and fear. She didn't like me because of my talent. She and my sisters all had lousy voices and they hated me for mine. When I review my lifelong financial problems, I have to admit they all began with Mother.'

The implication here is very clear: as Judy was still a minor it was Ethel who signed her contract with MGM, and Ethel who made sure that most of the money found its way to her. What happened to it after that is debatable. What is certain is that Judy became the 'cash cow' for the entire family, with the willing connivance of L.B. Mayer and the rest of MGM. Nobody apparently even once suggested a vacation or a break for the adolescent girl whose growing body was a constant source of misery to her. Short on praise, she was constantly berated for being overweight. Since Judy never had any money of her own, she was never taught how to handle it, and her apparent profligacy and bad financial judgement in later life can be dated to this early parental mistake.

As both her schooling and her career were totally governed by MGM, and her cross-country tours heavily chaperoned, Judy never had the chance to discover the teenage world inhabited by others.

The contrast between the screen persona of the bright and bubbly, if still somewhat chubby, youngster and the reality of an amphetamine-altered musical robot going from cinema to cinema, either on tour or on celluloid, was already painfully apparent to Roger Edens and the few other concerned grown-ups around the MGM lot; none of them, however, had the power or the motivation to do anything really useful to help. That would have meant standing up to Louis B. Mayer and Ethel Gumm, a far too potent combination for anyone who still had a living to make at Metro. Moreover, the studio was still not willing, as it had been with their other two contract child stars, Freddie Bartholomew and Mickey Rooney, to build a film around her alone.

Having already paired her once with Rooney (*Thoroughbreds Don't Cry*), they now tried her with Bartholomew for her third film of 1938. *Listen, Darling* was notable for Mary Astor (who was again to play Judy's mother in *Meet Me In St Louis* six years later) and for Walter Pidgeon as the adults. But the best thing about what the *New York Times* called 'a natural, pleasant, sensible and winsome little film' was that Judy got to sing for the first time one of her great standards, 'Zing Went the Strings of my Heart'. There really was not a lot more to be said about *Listen, Darling*, and as soon as her scenes were complete, Judy was immediately transferred to the fourth in Metro's longest-running and most triumphant series.

LEFT *Judy in the 'Swing Mr Mendelssohn' number from* Everybody Sing *(1938)*. ☆

RIGHT *Judy celebrating her* New Pair of Shoes *in* Thoroughbreds Don't Cry *(1937).* ☆

The Andy Hardy sequence had started in 1937 with *A Family Affair* and continued the following year with *Judge Hardy's Children*. These had established the stardom of Mickey Rooney who, as he said, was to be 'a fourteen-year old boy for at least thirty years'. But it wasn't until Judy joined him that the series really took off.

Love Finds Andy Hardy was far and away the best of the sequence, but it was still quite clearly a vehicle for Rooney. The plot simply lined up Garland, Ann Rutherford and Metro's newest young redhead, Lana Turner, all of whom dawdled around on-screen until Rooney made his choice.

As far as 'Uncle' Louis B. Mayer was concerned, the Garland agenda was now perfectly clear. Furious that Deanna Durbin had chosen to go to Universal, he had taken to announcing to all who would listen, 'I'll make the fat kid bigger than Deanna.' To visitors on any of Judy's sets, he would go even further. 'Do you see that girl?' he would proudly ask. 'She used to be a hunchback and now she's the greatest musical comedy star on our lot.'

It was her sister Virginia who later recalled the beginning of what could already be seen as Judy's end: 'There are times, at a place like Metro, when they don't give a damn about your talent – all they worry about is how you look, and they make a big thing out of that. This was just the time when Benzedrine and stuff like that first came out, and nobody thought it could be bad. It just killed your appetite, and that's why you took it. Nobody

realized it was Speed. The studio doctor gave her Dexedrine, I think, to keep her weight down. But you have to remember that nobody thought it was bad – certainly our mother didn't understand, and if she had, she would not have let Judy take it, but in those days nobody knew anything about these new drugs except that they seemed to be some kind of miracle-workers.'

Judy, lacking a sense of family and constantly aware that her mother saw her as nothing more than a meal ticket, was always looking for a way to please. She loved to eat – for comfort if not for the taste of it – but was not, in fact, fat, despite Mayer's frequently disparaging remarks on the subject. But celluloid, combined with the very strong lighting that was thought at the time to make young people look even younger than they were, also made her look fatter than she was, so that she looked, on-screen, as though she weighed about ten pounds more than she did.

On the other hand, Mayer's influence over Judy, and her mother's eagerness to please him have often been overestimated, as has the likelihood that old 'Uncle' Louis ever took the teenage Judy to bed, a rumour very much in circulation at the time. In truth, Judy was sufficiently established by now on both radio and film for her mother to have been able to take her to another studio if she had wanted to, and although there seems to be evidence that someone around the studio took Judy to bed well before her sixteenth birthday, the evidence no longer

points to Mayer. Losing her virginity was certainly in Judy's plan, and there is no question that, as a little girl constantly being told she was fat and ugly and still unable to make her own decisions (although clearly being worked as hard as any adult), the fact that she was desired as a woman and not found to be too unattractive to make love, was high on her list of desirable outcomes. This was no blushing violet, nor violated maiden, but a young woman anxious to demonstrate to herself, if to nobody else, that she was grown-up and wanted.

And as early as this, in May 1938, a month before her sixteenth birthday, Garland's reputation for being either unlucky or unreliable or plain un-cooperative on the set was already starting. Being driven home from the studio one night, she got into a car crash which left her with three broken ribs, a sprained back and a punctured lung. MGM, as so often in the future, immediately began casting around for a replacement, but at least now Judy was strong enough to overcome such setbacks, and within two weeks she was back on the set and had pre-recorded all four of her songs.

In the view of several critics, Judy came close to stealing *Love Finds Andy Hardy* from the irrepress-ible Rooney. Meanwhile life in the little red schoolroom and on the various lots at MGM was still far from ideal. 'Oh sure', Judy once reflected, 'those early days at MGM were a lot of laughs, but we were all young and frightened and we stayed frightened. Look at what happened to us – Mickey Rooney,

Lana Turner, Elizabeth Taylor and me – we all came out of there a little ticky and very kooky.'

Precisely because Judy now had this whole other life on live coast-to-coast radio broadcasts every Sunday, it was to the musical men at MGM that she really most appealed. Roger Edens, the arranger, and Arthur Freed, the songwriter and head of the Metro Musicals unit, were already aware that if Judy could be nursed into musicals, she would find her real audience.

Meanwhile, there was still the constant worry over her weight. All through her life she would prove capable of putting on as much as twenty pounds in a few days without even trying and, as one studio executive remembered of Judy at this time, 'She had all the characteristics of a chipmunk; she hated to sit still, her bright eyes were always on the alert for fun or danger, she resented being caged by the studio, and she was forever greedily searching for something to eat. The canteen staff had strict orders only to bring her cottage cheese and clear soup, so, like the chipmunk, she was always searching for places where she could tuck away a cookie, a chocolate bar, or sometimes a whole cake.'

Judy herself was later to flag the disastrous consequences that started here: 'I starved my appetite. I starved my system. I began, for the first time in my life, to suffer moods of absolute depression. Remembering how happy I had been as a child in vaudeville, I couldn't understand how unhappy I was as a teenager around the studios.' The pity is

that her weight, even when she gained a few pounds, was not excessive by any but movie standards.

MGM publicists were now starting to work on the Garland image. At sixteen, they decided, she was already too old to be a child star, so they began to announce that she was a mere fourteen and to give her, whenever she went on the road to sell her movies, a whole press pack of lies. Yes, she had been discovered singing at Lake Tahoe; no, she did not wish to be an actress when she grew up but was thinking seriously of nursing. In truth, what she had going for her, apart from that amazingly adult voice, was a real talent for comedy which thus far had been kept well hidden from the cameras. Working with Rooney, himself a brilliant mimic, she could match him parody for parody. In the endless waits between takes, he would do Carmen Miranda, Harry Lauder and Lionel Barrymore, while she

would do Sarah Bernhardt dying, Gertrude Lawrence taking off her gloves, or Maurice Chevalier, using a white fruit bowl for a straw hat. Judy's first crush was of course on Mickey but, as she was to say later, 'I always have to have a crush on somebody and they never ever last.'

In the November of 1937, when Judy had *Broadway Melody of 1938*, *Thoroughbreds Don't Cry* and *Everybody Sing* all doing well on general release, Arthur Freed went for a working breakfast with Louis B. Mayer at his Malibu beach house. Freed was now keen to establish his own empire within MGM, and very soon he was to bring to the studio such gifted musical talents as those of Gene Kelly, Busby Berkeley and Vincente Minnelli. In demanding that Mayer promote him from songwriter to producer, he also told the studio chief that he had another idea.

4. We're Off To See The Wizard

1938

Back in 1899, a failed actor, playwright, and machine-oil salesman called L. Frank Baum (the L, a little-known fact, stood for Lyman), who already owned a weekly newspaper and a ten-cent store, sent to the Chicago publisher, George M. Hill, the first draft of a book he wanted to call *The Emerald City*. When it appeared in print a year later, it sold out 100,000 copies within its first few months as *The Wonderful Wizard of Oz*. A year later, Baum himself had turned it into a five-act children's operetta which, for stage longevity, was only beaten in the first twenty years of this century by *The Merry Widow* and *Floradora*.

> 'You see that girl? She used to be a hunchback and now she's the greatest musical comedy star on our lot'
> Louis B. Mayer

RIGHT *Not yet a long way from Kansas – Judy in the black and white opening to* The Wizard of Oz *(1939).* ☆

Like such other timeless children's classics as *Mary Poppins* and *Dr Dolittle*, *The Wizard of Oz* was never a single novel but rather a series of short stories which were taken together, nearly always by other hands, and turned into a unified whole.

In this case, the stories almost all concerned a little girl called Dorothy with a vaguely unhappy home life who gets swept by a whirlwind into a magical kingdom full of midgets, witches good and evil, a tin man, a scarecrow, a cowardly lion and an apparently omnipotent wizard who turns out to be nothing more than a confidence trickster.

Two silent films had already been made in 1910 and 1925, the second of which starred Oliver Hardy. Now, in 1938, Samuel Goldwyn sold off the remaining movie rights to MGM for $20,000, a high advance for the time, reflecting general awareness that there was still a good deal of screen life to be found in the Emerald City.

Baum, in his original preface, had been quite clear about what he was trying to do: 'I have deliberately eliminated all the horrible and blood-curdling incidents of the standard fairy tale; mine aspires to be a modern one, in which the wonderment and joy are retained and the heartaches and nightmares are left out.' But, in point of fact, *Oz* does draw on a number of the timeless elements of the fairy-tale: it is not too difficult to see Dorothy as Cinderella, the Wicked Witch as the evil step-mother, and the Tin Man, Lion and Scarecrow as distant cousins of the Buttons who always comes to Cinders' rescue in pantomime. More contemporary followers of Stephen Sondheim's *Into the Woods* could even argue that the old fraudulent Wizard is simply a veteran version of the Princes Charming who always turn out (at least in Sondheim) to be nothing more than charming.

You could also, were you so minded, find in *The Wizard of Oz* strong parallels with the nearly contemporary British *Peter Pan*, in which J.M. Barrie also creates a Neverland to which a young girl (in his case Wendy) flies off in search of some sort of fulfilment.

Like the Neverland, Oz remains a country and a climate and a culture still central to the fantasies of children of all ages. As recently as the 1990s, new Oz novels were still being published and it is arguable that John Boorman's futurist science-fiction *Zardoz* (1974) is, in the last two letters of its title, paying yet another deliberate tribute to Baum's undiminishing impact and influence.

By the time that the screen rights found their way to MGM, both *The Wizard of Oz* and *Peter Pan* had been in the public consciousness for almost forty years. Both, at the last, deliver the same message – that there's no place like home – and it was a message that appealed not only to the saccharine-and-schmaltz heart of Louis B. Mayer (who as an immigrant from Eastern Europe had never had a home) but also to a world which was again on the brink of war. Within a year or two of the movie's release, RAF pilots were already using

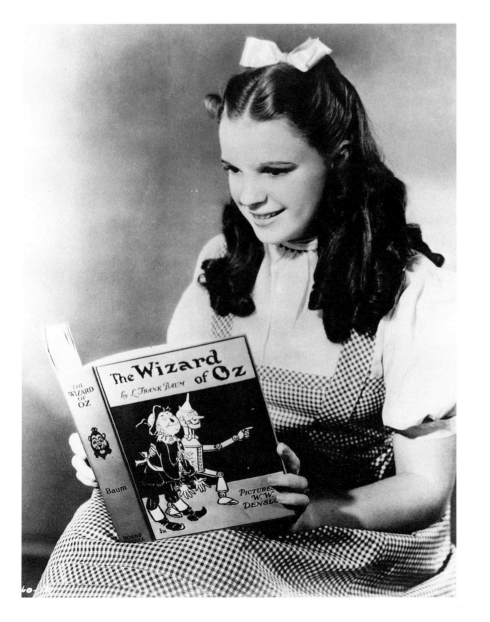

'We're Off to See the Wizard' as their theme song as they took off to attack the Luftwaffe.

In the sixty years since *The Wizard of Oz* first hit the cinemas, movie historians have endlessly argued over whether in fact it was the would-be producer Arthur Freed, or the eventual producer Mervyn LeRoy, who had first persuaded Mayer to acquire the rights but, in the end, all that matters is that the movie did get made. Curiously, like *Casablanca*, it was by no means an overnight success. It took the coming of television in the 1950s and the subsequent endless reruns on the small screen to turn both movies into the classics they have now become.

Even now, however, as their first ideas about the casting of the first talking *Wizard of Oz* were beginning to be aired by Freed and Mayer and LeRoy, Judy Garland was by no means at the head of their wish list for Dorothy. Still irritated by the way he had allowed Deanna Durbin to slip through his fingers and become a star elsewhere, Mayer was still not convinced that his 'little hunchback' could take her place. In virtually all her previous MGM roles, Judy had been freckled and frumpish; the feeling was that Shirley Temple would be much better insurance at the box-office. True, she was still only ten years old, but for three consecutive years (1935, 1936, and 1937) now she had topped all box-office charts. If Shirley had been available for the role, she would certainly have got it. Happily for Judy, and for us, Darryl Zanuck simply refused to lend her out from her contract with 20th Century Fox. A year later, by which time he and little Shirley had realized their ghastly mistake, they made a version of Maeterlinck's *The Bluebird* which was bad enough effectively to end her career – even the kindest critics referred to it as 'The Dead Pigeon'.

By default, therefore, Judy now had the role of her lifetime, but the rest of the casting did not come so easily. Ray Bolger, an MGM contract player, badly wanted to play the Scarecrow but was originally cast as the Tin Man: Buddy Ebsen, then a song-and-dance-man but later famous for *Breakfast at Tiffany's*, *The Beverly Hillbillies* and *Barnaby Jones*, was the first choice for the Scarecrow until the two actors were allowed to switch. Even that wasn't the end of the matter. Ten days into the shooting, Ebsen got an eye infection from the Tin Man's tin costume and had to be replaced by Jack Haley. There were several others who also never made the final cut. The Good Witch, who was eventually played by Binnie Barnes, was first going to be Fannie Brice, while Edna May Oliver, originally cast as the Wicked Witch, was first replaced by Gale Sondergaard before the final choice was made for Margaret Hamilton.

Only on the casting of the Cowardly Lion was everyone agreed from the outset. His character was no longer (as in the Baum stories) that of a Prince in disguise. The screenwriter Noel Langley, now on his fourth draft, had decided that the Cowardly Lion would be just that, and the lyricist Yip Harburg, who regularly worked with Bert Lahr on Broadway, was convinced that, if he could sell him to MGM for the role, there would be at least one great Harburg lyric in the movie.

The *New Yorker* critic, John Lahr, writing about his father in one of the greatest of all theatrical biographies – *Notes on a Cowardly Lion* – recalled that his father's pre-*Wizard* movie career had been nothing to write home about. Two studios (20th Century Fox and Universal) had already failed to renew his brief contracts there, and the general feeling around Hollywood was that Lahr was too grotesque, too vaudeville, too Broadway, ever to make it in the more intimate confines of a film studio. Only when disguised as the Cowardly Lion did Bert Lahr really find himself at home in a movie, and although he lived and worked on stage for another thirty years, finishing up in a definitive *Waiting For Godot*, he was never again to find a role that so perfectly fitted his outsize talents. 'After *The Wizard of Oz*,' Bert said laconically, 'I was typecast as a lion, and there aren't all that many parts for lions.'

By February 1938, MGM was able to announce that Judy Garland would be starring in a new production of *The Wizard of Oz*, budgeted at an astronomical and almost unprecedented $3,500,000. At first it was hoped that Busby Berkeley would choreograph the musical numbers, and among the early directors of choice were Norman Taurog and Richard Thorpe.

RIGHT *With Ray Bolger as the Scarecrow as they set off on the Yellow Brick Road to Oz.* ☆

Thorpe actually started shooting on 13 October 1938, but after less than a week it was felt that his rushes lacked fantasy and charm. LeRoy was still begging to take over, but Mayer, always his own man, went instead to George Cukor (who survived just two days) and then Victor Fleming, who was the original director of record, although he too left the project to replace Cukor on *Gone with the Wind*.

Precisely who could therefore be called the director of *The Wizard of Oz* is a moot point. Fleming was certainly responsible for most of the footage and is, indeed, the only credited director. When he was summoned to Tara, however, it was probably Mervyn LeRoy who, having wrested the producer title from Arthur Freed, actually finished the picture as he always believed God intended. What is less well known is that the black-and-white sequences which open and close the film were the work of none of them. They were directed by the already veteran King Vidor.

As was then the custom with all MGM musicals, the complete score by Harburg with music by Harold Arlen was pre-recorded under the direction of Roger Edens. A dozen numbers, including 'If I Only Had A Heart', 'If I Were King of the Forest', 'The Jitterbug Dance' (only recently restored to the movie) and, of course, the signature song 'Over The Rainbow' were just a few of the reasons why this film was to connect so directly with the hearts of its audience.

Even with the score in the can, however, *The Wizard of Oz* was not yet quite ready to shoot. One of its central problems was the plot's demand for 150 dwarfs to play the Munchkin midgets. The call went out all over America and the response was overwhelming. Those selected were bussed into New York for final auditions. Those finally chosen were then loaded on to buses whose drivers had orders to deliver them safely to Hollywood, where shooting was about to start. A few minutes after their departure, the head of the MGM casting department gaped in horror out of his Plaza Hotel suite to see four busloads of dwarfs proceeding slowly down Fifth Avenue in the wrong direction with their naked posteriors sticking out of all the windows.

'Quite soon,' recalled Fleming, 'those damn Munchkins were all over the lot. They were so darn small, and their costumes were all the same, so when they mobbed together they were just a vast mass of nothing. They were also the most deformed and unpleasant bunch of adults imaginable. Within days MGM's Culver City was crawling with them. They propositioned everybody; in the commissary, always filled to capacity at lunchtime, they were always getting under your feet. This unholy assembly of pimps, hookers and gamblers infested MGM like rats.'

They also drank uncontrollably, held all-night parties of unbelievable depravity in their hotels (where a full-time lavatory attendant had to be employed in the men's room merely to lift Munchkins on to toilet seats) and made outrageous union demands. Those few left alive who worked with them on the picture have only to hear the word 'Munchkin' to dissolve into total nervous collapse, and there is at least one novel and one whole movie about the chaos into which the Munchkins hurled Metro. Whenever a kindly gate-keeper or executive would bend condescendingly toward one of them and ask, 'And how are you, my little man?' the standard Munchkin reply was, invariably, 'Go fuck yourself.'

And there was just one more little problem. Technicolor was then in its infancy and mainly being developed by David Selznick for the contemporaneous *Gone with the Wind*. Indeed rights for the new process had to be sub-leased from him. But it was Victor Fleming, working simultaneously on both movies, who had the brainwave of shooting the 'real' Kansas footage in black-and-white and the 'fantasy' scenes of Oz in brilliant Technicolor. Like all new processes, it worked sometimes. The schedule, already budgeted higher than the average film, was nonetheless drawn out by the twin nightmares of its technical and logistical demands. The cast was enormous and frequently uncontrollable, while the colour technicians had needs of their own which had never been envisaged.

After 136 days (extended because Judy was already becoming slightly unreliable, for a variety of real and imagined ailments) principal photography was completed on 16 March 1939. Judy was at once thrown into her next Mickey Rooney picture, *Babes in Arms*, but Victor Fleming now began to work a nightmare schedule, directing *Gone with the Wind* all day and editing *The Wizard of Oz* all night.

When Judy Garland first sang 'Over the Rainbow', with its universal, heart-breaking, unanswerable query, 'Why, oh why, can't I?', she was all of sixteen years old. When she was found dead, sitting on a London lavatory, almost exactly thirty years later, every single obituary all over the world linked her to that song, a song that almost didn't exist.

At the first sneak preview in the autumn of 1939, Mayer insisted that it be removed. Why, he asked Harburg and Arlen unanswerably, is there a girl singing in a farmyard? The song was missing from several early prints. It was only permanently restored to the final cut months later, by which time Freed had convinced Mayer of his mistake.

Towards the end of her short and unhappy life, Judy would dwell in interviews on how miserable she had been at Metro even as early as *The Wizard of Oz*. But her memories did not reflect those of the rest of the cast, who found her 'enchanting', 'light-hearted', 'always laughing', 'perfectly mannered' and 'cheery and bright and a joy to be around'.

The only memory of any kind of teenage sadness came from Margaret Hamilton, who remembered Judy rather wistfully remarking that she had never had the chance to do the things or make the friends that 'ordinary' little girls took for granted.

Judy would later also claim that the three old vaudevillians – Bolger, Haley and Lahr – were forever upstaging her and driving her to the edges of the screen. But this is not borne out by any viewing of the picture, where she is nearly always found in the middle of their group, nor by the memory of Victor Fleming who every day, he said, would remind the trio of old stage pros that they were to be especially generous and thoughtful to their little girl. Of course, if he particularly remembers that he had to be firm with them on the subject, the probability is that he was noticing at least something that suggested they were not being too generous towards her. Indeed, one of the most familiar sounds on the *Oz* set was of Fleming, high on a camera crane, screaming down, 'You three dirty hams, let the little girl in there.'

It was during the shooting of *The Wizard of Oz* in 1939 that Judy started on her first grand passion. The man was an already twice-divorced jazz clarinettist and bandleader by the name of Artie Shaw, and Judy's unrequited love for him was, if anything, heightened by the fact that early in their relationship Shaw was rushed to hospital and almost died of a form of leukaemia. Judy would spend every moment that she wasn't being Dorothy by his bedside, and although he saw her as the little sister he never had, there is no doubt that she longed for a sexual relationship with him which, despite his enthusiastic womanizing elsewhere, was never to happen.

Judy and her mother had just built themselves, on the proceeds of her MGM salary, a large four-bedroom house on Stone Canyon Road in West Los Angeles, and it was there, with such buddies as the jazz drummer Buddy Rich and the comic Phil Silvers, that Artie Shaw would now spend more and more of his time.

The relationship with Shaw now became effectively that of Professor Higgins and Eliza Dolittle. Although Shaw had so murky a sexual reputation that the parents of every Hollywood girl were forever trying to ban him from their doors (including Jerome Kern, who totally failed to stop him eloping with and marrying his adored only child, Betty), as far as Judy was concerned, Artie was unusually content just to teach her everything he knew. And he knew a lot; about books, about music, about a whole outside and adult world into which Judy was now only very tentatively and briefly emerging.

Professionally, perhaps the most important thing that Artie Shaw did for Judy in the few months that they were together was to introduce her to the pianist/composer Oscar Levant and the lyricist Ira Gershwin, who was still mourning the recent death of Ira's brother George. It was of course Ira who, a dozen years later, was to give Judy her last great score for *A Star is Born*, but for now, it was at Ira and Leonore Gershwin's house on North Roxbury Drive, with its two famous pianos and its tennis courts, that Judy at

last began to feel at home, as well as at work, in Hollywood.

Apart from Shaw, Judy's regular escorts now included Mickey Rooney, the actor Peter Lind Hays, and even Groucho Marx, but she was effectively adopted both by the Gershwins and the Levants, and with them her social life began to improve exponentially.

Only three weeks before the outbreak of war in Europe, *The Wizard of Oz* had its world premiere at Loew's Capitol in New York. It was attended by Judy and her mother and a vast gathering of MGM studio stars but also, more importantly, by Mickey Rooney, who had just been declared the number one box-office draw in all America.

For the first month of that initial movie run on Broadway, Judy and Mickey, in between the screenings, would do four live acts a day. And this at a time when she had gone straight from *The Wizard of Oz* to *Babes in Arms* without a single week's vacation. Not surprisingly, this was the first (but sadly by no means the last) occasion on which Judy collapsed backstage. She slumped and fainted in the wings, some said out of sheer exhaustion and others because of her diet, which now seemed to consist entirely of Coca Cola. She was back on stage the following day and, with its customary disregard for her mental or physical welfare, the studio immediately announced that, following the New York stage engagement and before her next movie, Garland and Rooney would do personal appearances

LEFT *At the gates of The Emerald City.* ☆

with their current releases in five other cities, as well as judging teenage talent contests in a further seventy cinemas.

Privately, her life was also now seriously disturbed by two events. Her mother left the house in Stone Canyon to elope with her lover, Will Gillmore. This was an act of betrayal to her father which Judy never forgave, because Ethel had married him in 1935, perhaps not coincidentally, on the anniversary of her first husband's death.

The second blow was the sudden illness of her friend and confidant Artie Shaw, who disappeared from her life into a serious nervous breakdown at the time when she most needed him. As was to happen again so many times in her future, the exhaustion of her public responsibilities had coincided with the despair of her private life, and there was just nobody there to support or help her get through the hard times.

But now at least she had *The Wizard of Oz* and, to misquote one of the best lyrics of her friend, Ira Gershwin, they couldn't take that away from her. We must always remember, however, that *The Wizard of Oz* then is not *The Wizard of Oz* now.

In Tom Stoppard's play *Travesties* there is a moment when the central character's wife is berating him for having failed to realize that one of his fellow players in a 1912 amateur Zurich staging of *The Importance of Being Earnest* was in fact Vladimir Ilyich Lenin. Ah, says her husband, but he wasn't Lenin *then*. In 1939 *The Wizard of Oz* was

just one major release in the year that can now be seen as the greatest in the whole century of cinema. Other movies either produced or released in 1939 include: *Gone With the Wind*, *Le Jour se Lève*, *Only Angels Have Wings*, Greta Garbo's *Ninotchka*, George Cukor's *The Women*, Frank Capra's *Mr Smith Goes To Washington*, John Ford's *Drums Along the Mohawk*, *Wuthering Heights*, *Goodbye, Mr Chips*, *Stagecoach*, *The Rules of the Game*, *Beau Geste*, Basil Rathbone's first Sherlock Holmes (*The Hound of the Baskervilles*), Ingrid Bergman's Hollywood debut (*Intermezzo*), Henry Fonda's *Young Mr Lincoln* and Hitchcock's *Rebecca*.

So, against this background, it is not surprising that *The Wizard of Oz* did not critically come into its own until a re-release in the much thinner year of 1948. Commercially, of course, it was always a huge hit. On the day of the first showing alone 37,000 people went to see it, but on its budget of $3,500,000 it made an initial studio loss of nearly a million dollars. The picture did not break even until 1948, ten full years later, and, by the weird ways of Hollywood accountants, it did not show a profit until the first television deal was made in 1976. Within another ten years the picture had brought back to MGM $34,000,000 in television rights, while video cassette sales worldwide are already well above $3,000,000.

The initial reviews were at best 'mixed'. Perhaps aware that the picture had been through no fewer than nine screenwriters before Noel Langley, not to mention four directors, many critics took the view that the original tales had been somehow betrayed by the decision to frame them within Dorothy's fantasy, brought about by being hit on the head during a Kansas 'twister'.

As usual, the cast were the first to get the movie into perspective, 'Nobody told us,' said Jack Haley, 'that we were supposed to be making a classic. It was a job. We were getting paid and it was simply a lot of weeks of steady work.' As for Margaret Hamilton, she remembered the initial reviews as 'very pleasant but not by any means what we in the business would call Money Reviews.'

One of the most thoughtful reviews came, as usual, from Otis Ferguson for the *New Republic*: '*The Wizard of Oz* is clearly intended to hit the same audience as *Snow White*, and it won't fail for lack of trying. It has dwarfs, music, Technicolor, freak characters and Judy Garland. It can't be expected to have a sense of humour as well, and as for the light touch of fantasy, it weighs like a pound of fruitcake soaking wet. Children will not object to it, especially as it is a thing of many interesting gadgets; but it will be delightful for children mostly with their mothers, while any kid tall enough to reach up to the ticket window will be down the street booking for the latest *Tarzan*.

'The story of course has some lovely and wild ideas, men of straw and tin, a cowardly lion, a wizard who isn't a very good wizard, but the picture doesn't know what to do with them, except to be painfully literal and elaborate about everything; Cecil B. de Mille and the Seven Thousand Dwarfs, as it were. As for Judy Garland, it isn't that this little slip of a miss spoils the fantasy, so much as that her thumping, overgrown gambols are characteristic of its treatment here. When she is merry, the house shakes, and when she is forlorn everybody gets wet.'

In Britain, Graham Greene noted: 'The whole picture is incredible lavish and there's a lot of pleasure to be got these days from watching money spent on other things than war… but to us, in our old tribal continent, the morality here seems a little crude and the fancy material rattles like dry goods … The author of this fantasy was always the agile salesman, offering his customers the best of material dreams … but if we regard this picture as a pantomime, it has good moments – the songs are charming, the Technicolor no more dreadful than the illustrations to most children's books, and the sepia prologue on the Kansas plains, when the child runs away from home to save her dog from a spinster neighbour and the tornado comes twisting across the horizon, is very fine indeed. As for Miss Judy Garland, with her delectable long-legged stride, she would have won one's heart for a whole winter's season twenty years ago.'

In the *New Yorker*, Russell Maloney took the view that 'Fantasy is still the undisputed domain of Walt Disney. Nobody else can tell a fairy-tale with his clarity of imagination, his supple good taste or

his technical ingenuity; this was forcibly borne in on me as I sat cringing before MGM's Technicolor production of *The Wizard of Oz* which displays no trace of imagination, good taste or ingenuity. The film is a stinkeroo.'

This was not the view of any post-war critic, but in 1939 when *Oz* had begun to acquire its addicts, not least the reviewer of the *New York Times* who wrote of 'a fairybook tale told in fairybook style with witches, goblins, pixies and other wondrous things drawn in the brightest colours. It is all so well-intentioned, so genial and so gay that any reviewer who would look down his nose at the fun-making here should be spanked and sent off, supperless to bed.'

One issue that no critic has yet faced head on is precisely how and when and why *The Wizard of Oz* became a gay landmark; it probably started around the late 1950s and early 60s when Judy herself was drawing large crowds of gays in America and especially Europe to her concert appearances, wherein she had taken on the role of the 'doomed diva' hitherto played by both Maria Callas and Edith Piaf. Around that time, if not before, the phrase 'a friend of Dorothy's' became gay code for 'one of us', while 'We're a long way from Kansas, Toto' also became a high-camp phrase on the cabaret circuit.

But it is not hard to fathom why, into and even after the first great AIDS plague, the idea of having somewhere over the rainbow where things were organized differently for nonconformists should have become so attractive to a socially and sexually threatened community. Moreover Dorothy's cry of 'Why, oh why, can't I?' reinforces the idea of the impossible dream and the unattainable magic city where we shall all be given hearts and brains and courage to face an uncertain future.

In fact, of course, this was the precise opposite of the message that Louis B. Mayer wanted his *Wizard* to deliver; in 1939 the idea of there being 'no place like home' perfectly suited American pre-war isolationism. It was only long after the war that home became synonymous with a place where mother didn't understand about your boy-friend if you were male, and where the family had to be sheltered from the reality of sexually trans-mitted diseases. Suddenly Oz then becomes the magic land, and home is for escaping from; but if old uncle Louis B. Mayer had ever suspected that he was making a film which would eventually become a gay classic, he might easily have pulled it from the studio schedules in a fit of homophobic terror and rage. The whirligig of time, as Feste notes in *Twelfth Night*, does indeed bring in its revenges.

LEFT *Judy and her mother Ethel making the best of a bad relationship for an MGM fan magazine.* ☆

5. Babe In Arms: Judy Goes to War

1939—1943

Weeks before the release of *The Wizard of Oz*, Judy was already back at work (as per her Metro contract) on *Babes in Arms*, the third of the ten films she was to make with Mickey Rooney. It was also the one which finally brought her together with the director and choreographer Busby Berkeley, and although it was still a vehicle for Rooney it was the first in which she achieved co-star billing and at least reasonable parity in the song-and-dance routines.

'How could I ignore the boy next door?'

RIGHT *Hearts of Oak: Judy and Mickey as the* Babes in Arms *(1939).* ☆

The script, such as it was, contained for the first time the immortal line, 'Hey, let's put on the show right here', and the score included a vast range of numbers, among them the amazing neo-Fascist torchlight marching song that gave the film its title, as well as the first use of Arthur Freed and Nacio Herb Brown's 'Good Morning', repeated twelve years later to much better effect by Gene Kelly, Donald O'Connor and Debbie Reynolds in *Singin' in the Rain*.

Indeed the score of *Babes in Arms* also featured songs by Rodgers and Hart (the original writers of the stage musical on which it was based), as well as Harold Arlen and Yip Harburg, making it as diffuse and disjointed as the plot, which was loosely about a couple of teenagers trying to prove that they are as good as a group of old-time vaudevillians. When a has-been old child star (June Preisser, looking, as a kind of in-joke, alarmingly like Shirley Temple) puts money into the show hoping to make a comeback, it is of course Garland's songs that she steals, thereby allowing Judy to sing a lament to a photograph – not this time of Clark Gable but of Mickey Rooney.

A deeply eccentric storyline ends up with one of the most expensive and truly bizarre sequences MGM had yet made: a nine-minute patriotic chant by Harburg and Arlen called 'God's Country', which concludes with the immortal pre-war couplet:

We've got no Duce and we've got not Fuhrer
But we got Garbo and Norma Shearer

Although both Judy and Mickey were soon to return to the tried and tested Andy Hardy format, *Babes in Arms* was clearly an intelligent attempt by MGM to see what else they could do together. And already the partnership that had started with a couple of kids was growing beyond adolescence. What they had in common was not just their age, but a kind of relentless perky optimism which was always interrupted by the moment when Judy thinks she has lost him for ever.

One of the best sequences in *Babes in Arms* had Rooney as FDR and Judy as Eleanor Roosevelt, but it was cut from the final print because their shared talent for mimicry had produced a parody slightly too real for the comfort of a fiercely patriotic and jingoistic 1939 America.

Within twenty-four hours of completing *Babes in Arms* towards the end of 1939, Mickey and Judy were thrown into the next of the Andy Hardy sequence, *Andy Hardy Meets Debutante* – the latter, needless to say, not Garland. By now, as Judy later recalled, they were both in real trouble: 'MGM would give us pep-up pills to keep us on our feet long after we were exhausted. Then they would take us to the studio hospital and knock us cold with sleeping pills – Mickey sprawled out on one bed and me on another. Then, after four hours, they'd wake us up and give us the pep-up pills again so we could work another seventy-two hours in a row. Half of the time we were hanging from the ceiling, but it became a way of life for us.' Even allowing for Garland's

RIGHT *Mickey and Judy parodying Franklyn and Eleanor Roosevelt for Babes in Arms.* ☆

ABOVE *Orchestrator and composer Roger Edens at the piano.* ☆

LEFT *Judy and Mickey arm in arm once again.* ☆

habit in later life of exaggerating her studio woes, if even half her story is true, it suggests that she and Rooney would nowadays have legal grounds for claiming that they had been abused children.

But the studio now had a great deal riding on the survival of their young superstars. Though the Andy Hardy series could still be made relatively cheaply, *Babes in Arms* and their subsequent musical *Strike Up the Band* were to come in at around three-quarters of a million dollars each, unusually high budgets for movies that were not in the one-off category of *Gone with the Wind* or *The Wizard of Oz*. Front office lost no time in reminding Judy that Mickey was the real star of the team, that she was still dangerously inclined to overeat, and that she alone could always easily be replaced.

Judy was now seventeen and approaching the first Christmas of the war in Europe, one which was for the next two years to have remarkably little impact on studio life in Hollywood. Under the terms of a tough contract, she was still only earning $500 a week (less than a third of what Rooney was now making), and of that she faithfully handed over each week $250 to her mother and her loathed new stepfather. To say that she was not a happy bunny was to put it mildly, and even her private life after the Artie Shaw episode was also now dictated by a fierce combination of her mother and Mayer, who decided that a suitable escort would be the young actor Robert Stack. Although the pair were locked together through several studio premieres, there

was no flicker of romance on either side, and Judy was going home to West Hollywood every night to nobody more exciting than her German shepherds – the canine rather than human variety.

Her best friend at the studio, the gay orchestrator and composer Roger Edens, noted of Judy at this moment, 'She was beginning to look for the meaning of things, but with no real education it was a lot like stumbling about in a heavy fog.' Judy herself put it even more graphically: 'There are just so many things locked up in my head that I feel if there was a can opener which could open my brain, all these thinkings and feelings would gush out like some unstoppable watertap.'

Rooney later took a rather more optimistic view of Judy's character: 'For us, work and fun were inextricably interwoven. It was impossible to tell just where one ended and the other began. Our work was our fun and our fun was our work. Just like in our movies, we talked about my writing a musical comedy for her which would make Judy a Broadway star. Her timing was like that of a chronometer. She could deliver a comic line with just the right comic touch, or say a poignant line slowly enough for the poignancy to hit hard but still stay short of *schmaltz*. She and I could both turn on the intensity, memorize great chunks of script, and of course ad-lib when necessary. Alone, she could take a very ordinary scene and by the sheer strength of her talent, make it a scene that people everywhere would remember for ever.'

Hollywood's continuing uncertainty about precisely where or even how to fit Judy into their scheme of things was underlined early in 1940 by the award of her only Oscar. Whereas Rooney was nominated that year specifically for *Babes in Arms*, Judy won her Oscar not, as might surely have been expected, for Dorothy in *The Wizard of Oz* but in the totally sexless and unique category of Best Juvenile Performer. She did not therefore win in contest, but was simply handed a special miniature statue instead of the real thing. Rooney, incidentally, lost his that year to Robert Donat for *Goodbye, Mr Chips*, and at least ten of the other awards went, unsurprisingly, to *Gone with the Wind*.

On Oscar night itself, Garland met the young actor with whom she was to start her first (albeit very short-lived) adult affair. He was Tyrone Power, then twenty-six, almost ten years older than Judy and newly arrived at stardom as a result of his appearances in three recent major movies – *Marie Antoinette*, *In Old Chicago*, and *Alexander's Ragtime Band*. He had just the dark, handsome sexiness to appeal to a young girl still unsure of her own attractiveness and as yet untried in her own sexuality.

But she was still not even eighteen, and the moment their affair was noticed alarm bells rang loudly for both mother Ethel and 'Uncle' Louis. Both Charlie Chaplin and Errol Flynn had recently been in considerable career trouble for sexual activity with teenage jailbait, and both Garland

and Power were too hot to be allowed to make the same mistake. Their affair came to a near-farcical end a few weeks later when a prowler attempted to kidnap Judy from her home which, not surprisingly, unnerved her badly. Power, sensing her panic, decided that a short holiday would calm her and they agreed to go for a few days of comparative safety over the border into Mexico. Mayer promptly told the docile Hollywood police that Power was guilty of crossing the State line with an under-age girl, and only when they threatened to charge him on his return to California did Power understandably and perhaps even eagerly promise never to see her alone again.

The MGM hierarchy still treated Judy as though she were the daughter of a Victorian autocrat. It was Keenan Wynn who noted that every time an MGM executive opened his mouth dust would fall out, but the studio was still eager to create Garland in their own image. To this end, the resident publicist Howard Strickling published a twenty-five-page biography of Judy for the use of all journalists who came to interview her.

True, she was not a great interviewee at this time, and her studio biography was unintentionally a great deal funnier than she ever was off-screen. It included such information as the fact that her mother was teaching her to play the piano with the aid of a book entitled *Chopin in the Home*. It also announced that she always went to bed alone, but only after saying her prayers, and that,

RIGHT *Spot the* Ziegfeld Girl *(1941): Lana Turner, Judy, and Hedy Lamarr* ☆

apparently unique in the annals of Hollywood actresses, 'She always takes care of her own clothes and bedroom.'

The truth was rather different. Desperate to escape her mother and her detested new husband, and eager for some sort of a sex life, Judy was now counting the days until at eighteen she could legally set up her own accommodation. In the meantime, however, Lana Turner, though still a rung or three below Judy on the MGM ladder, had struck a double blow. Within a matter of weeks, she was the woman to whom Tyrone Power turned after his brief dalliance with Judy, and it was then Lana who married Garland's only other love, Artie Shaw, albeit only for four months. A depressed Judy was still condemned to the twin lives of unreality on the lot as Mickey Rooney's sidekick, and misery at home, trapped with her mother and stepfather and missing her sisters, who had married and were only occasionally in touch.

Judy and Mickey were now at the heart of not one but two triumphant MGM series, and they began to alternate the domestic Andy Hardy comedies with the musicals about streetwise kids doing the shows right there and then. *Andy Hardy Meets Debutante* did not risk any changes to the formula. Judy again played the small-town girl who worships Mickey but nearly loses him to a ritzier dame, and the rest of the plot, as if it mattered, turned on a court case in which Middle American values were upheld against those of a corrupt big-city aristocracy.

When he saw the first of the Andy Hardys, 'Uncle' Louis had memorably instructed his staff not to make them any better. He too had realized what Sam Goldwyn always knew, that nobody ever got rich overestimating the intelligence of the Great American Public. This was, for the record, only Judy's second Andy Hardy but already Mickey Rooney's ninth, and as soon as it was completed, the two of them were straight back into their second campus musical, *Strike Up the Band*. At the same time, lest anyone thought Judy's workload was still insufficient, she was signed over by MGM to a long-running regular Sunday night Bob Hope radio show which was broadcast live from Los Angeles. Thus her one notional weekly day off was spent rehearsing and performing too.

Strike Up the Band was a considerable improvement on *Babes in Arms*, and was again produced by Arthur Freed and directed by Busby Berkeley. It too, however, had a somewhat multifarious score, having been culled from the back catalogues of a variety of songwriters including Freed himself, Roger Edens and George and Ira Gershwin. This time the other star of the film was Paul Whiteman (plus orchestra) and the storyline was essentially that of Mickey as a drum-playing teenager trying to join the band.

The original Broadway show had been by the Gershwins, with a book by George S. Kaufman, but as usual precious little of that was left intact. As the critic of *Newsweek* noted, 'When MGM channelled the bounce and brashness of Rooney,

Garland, and a castful of precocious youngsters in to a musical called *Babes in Arms* last year, the coins clinked in box-offices all over America. *Strike Up the Band*, a second try in that exuberant groove, may lack the first film's spontaneity and zip but it should come close to matching its popularity … Undismayed now by the comprehensive competition of Rooney, Judy Garland does some monopolizing of her own with "Our Love Affair" and a handful of more dated favorites.'

Another critic was in no doubt about the potency of this movie's mission to entertain at all costs: 'This is the film they should show to Hitler – it might cheer even him up,' and Judy Garland's celebrated Conga was reckoned for the first time to establish her in full bloom beyond childhood. As yet another critic added, 'At long, long last, MGM has developed a leading woman who doesn't remind you of your mother.'

Off-screen, Judy was still deeply unhappy with her treatment. 'Sometimes I would get to bed at two in the morning and be awakened at five. They'd rush me into make-up, where I always thought they painted eyeballs on to my lids to make me look awake. In addition to the lack of sleep, my head was always buzzing with too many numbers, too many lyrics, too many dances, too much to learn.'

And now there was an additional problem. Judy had reached the moment when, like Shirley Temple and Mickey Rooney and Deanna Durbin just before her, she ached to become a woman on-screen, just

RIGHT *Mickey and Judy leading the Conga for* Strike Up the Band *(1940).* ☆

LEFT *Mickey gives Judy a lift in* Strike Up the Band. ☆

RIGHT *Judy wardrobe testing for* Little Nelly Kelly *(1940).* ☆

as she was becoming one in real life. For once, MGM (determined that nothing would keep her for too long away from the money-spinning Andy Hardy and the Rooney musicals) acceded to her request for the sake of peace and quiet and threw her into *Little Nellie Kelly*, the famous old George M. Cohan Broadway hit about the young Irish girl who marries the man she loves against the wishes of her father.

Deciding that the great American public was not yet ready for the shock of both Rooney and Garland in adult roles, they now paired her with George Murphy and moreover allowed her to play the dual role of his wife and daughter. Garland's reviews here were not bad, but nor were they especially good, and there was the strong sense of a young star being indulged rather than a serious breakthrough into dramatic roles. Judy may have got her first screen kiss here, but within weeks she was back as a showbiz teenager playing second fiddle to Lana Turner in *Ziegfeld Girl*.

Unusually, this was not a Freed/Berkeley production, but instead produced by Pandro Berman and directed by Robert Z. Leonard. Sharing the set with such glamour girls as Turner and Hedy Lamarr, Judy noted ruefully that whenever anyone passed the other two they would whistle appreciatively whereas, when they got to her, they just said 'Hi, Judy' and went their way.

Always with Garland it is crucial to separate the 'then' from the 'now'. Years later, her pianist/

arranger Roger Edens would call Garland's arrival at the studio 'The greatest thing ever to happen to the MGM musical', and the critic David Shipman would add, 'When the dream factory in full blast produced its masterpiece, that masterpiece was Judy.'

Yet at this time, early in 1940, Judy was still the chubby late teenager who had somehow failed to transmute into Lana Turner or Hedy Lamarr. There was, even after Dorothy went over the rainbow, a curious sense of disillusion over her – as though, despite her undeniable box-office takings, Metro itself shared in her doubts about herself. They only knew really what to do with her when she was dancing a few feet behind Mickey Rooney or playing the hometown girl to whom, as Andy Hardy, he would almost reluctantly return after a brief taste of forbidden fruit elsewhere.

And now, as if to confirm their belief that she could never really be credible as a 'Ziegfeld girl', Metro threw her straight back into the third and mercifully last of her Andy Hardy pictures. This one, *Life Begins for Andy Hardy* could, as *Time Magazine* noted, 'hardly be said to tax Miss Garland's talent in her usual role of the Rooney-smitten Betsy.' The only subtle difference here was that the National Legion of Decency, still functioning as some kind of unofficial censor for Hollywood, now changed the Hardy classification from 'appropriate entertainment for children' to 'unobjectionable for adults', thus presumably taking

note of Andy Hardy's breathtaking announcement in this eleventh picture of the series 'Father, I am a man.' Millions of fans still didn't believe they'd heard him right.

A sequel-crazed studio now decided that on the musical front Mickey and Judy could follow *Babes in Arms* with *Babes on Broadway* in which, not for the first time, Mickey writes a musical which, aided and abetted by a gang of keen buddies, he then takes to Broadway. Here, though, despite everything that Busby Berkeley could do to imply that this was just the same old *schtick*, it becomes quite clear that Judy is, wherever possible, pulling away from Mickey to try, however tentatively at first, to establish a solo-star identity of her own. For once, they were working with an original story, if only in the sense that *Babes on Broadway* had not previously been a stage musical. Arthur Freed brought in three songwriters, Burton Lane, Yip Harburg and Ralph Freed; Alexander Woollcott was hired for all of $5,000 to spend one day on the prologue; and, most significantly for Judy's later life, Vincente Minnelli was brought in to be Berkeley's choreographer. Minnelli's triumph here was the 'Ghost Theatre' number, which allowed Judy and Mickey to make public the parodies they had always perfected in private to while away the long between-takes pauses. Now she got to imitate Sarah Bernhardt and Fay Templeton on-screen, while Mickey gave his Carmen Miranda, Harry Lauder, George M. Cohan, and Cyrano de Bergerac. The

RIGHT *Glorifying the American Girl: Judy on the inevitable staircase for Ziegfeld Girl (1941).* ☆

1165-419

only problem about these sketches was the one they did in blackface. Not until the film was previewed and passed in total silence did Berkeley suddenly realize with horror that he had neglected to film Mickey and Judy getting into their black make-up and, as a result, the first audience hadn't the faintest idea it was them. A dressing-room scene was hastily shot and inserted before the second preview.

There was only one real surprise during the filming of *Babes on Broadway*, and it was the arrival of two identical telegrams on the desks of 'Uncle' Louis and Arthur Freed one Monday morning in July 1940. Datelined Las Vegas, Nevada, they read: 'I AM SO VERY VERY HAPPY STOP DAVE AND I WERE MARRIED THIS MORNING STOP PLEASE GIVE ME A LITTLE TIME AND I WILL BE BACK TO FINISH THE PICTURE WITH ONE TAKE ON EACH SCENE STOP LOVE JUDY.'

Apart from the hollow laughter which must have greeted her one-take promise, this was seriously bad news for MGM. Their dumpy little teenager with the crush on Mickey Rooney had overnight transformed herself into the wife of the conductor and composer David Rose. Judy had only met him a few weeks earlier in a radio studio, where she was doing her usual Sunday gig for Bob Hope and he was Tony Martin's musical director, but romance blossomed very quickly indeed, not least because of Judy's desperation to get away from her mother and Louis B. Mayer's dominance.

Even if they could deal with the idea of a married Judy, Rose would certainly not have been their first choice of bridegroom. Apart from the fact that he was recently divorced from the comedienne Martha Raye (at a time when even in Hollywood divorce carried a certain stigma), all that was really known about Rose was that he was English, with a touch of class, and had a passion for his electric train set. Ethel took an instant dislike to him, pointing out that both Judy's elder sisters were already in marital trouble and adding rather sadly, 'All I wish is for one of my girls to marry somebody with a slide rule instead of a slide trombone.' But Judy was now nineteen and of an age to marry without consent, at least in Nevada, and she had in any case gone ahead without consulting anyone.

In marked contrast to any of her four subsequent husbands, Rose remained totally detached from the Judy Garland industry. He earned his own money, demanded separate bank accounts, and had taken the somewhat laid-back view that if Judy really wanted to get married, that was just fine by him.

However, the marriage lasted barely eight months, although the divorce was not sought until after the war. Rose, again in contrast to all his successors, was never to speak publicly either about the marriage or its rapid collapse. What is certain is that at nineteen Judy was not ready to run a house or staff, or indeed be any kind of a wife, and although she quickly became pregnant, there was an inevitable abortion on the instructions of the

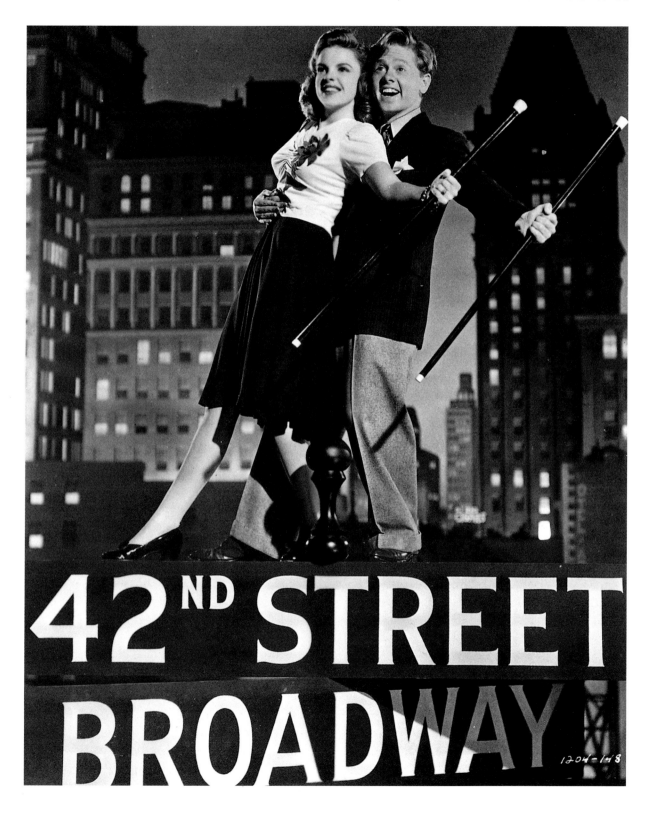

RIGHT *Judy and Mickey as the* Babes on Broadway *(1941).* ☆

studio. In those days there was total Hollywood acceptance of the theory that the girl could have a baby or a career but certainly not both.

Sometime later, a letter from Judy was discovered to throw at least some light on their problem. 'I'm miserable,' she wrote to a friend, 'Dave is at his music all night and I really can't blame him for that, as I'm at the studio all day. I wish I could say that he was a son of a bitch, but he certainly isn't. I wish he would do something so that I could put the blame on him but I can't – he is just so nice and I am just so miserable.'

Whether it was the abortion, or the conflicting work schedules, or just a simple drifting apart, the marriage was over to all intents and purposes even before David Rose joined the army soon after Pearl Harbor. The war effectively permitted them to separate without attracting any press attention, and their marriage ended in a June 1945 divorce as quietly as it had begun.

And meanwhile there was to be at least one other challenger for her attention in the lithe and sexy shape of a young Broadway hoofer newly arrived in Hollywood called Gene Kelly.

Kelly, now twenty-eight, had made his name overnight a year earlier as Pal Joey in Rodgers and Hart's landmark Broadway musical of the same name. For the first time, a heel had been made into a hero or, better still, an anti-hero. The show took the usually soft-focus romantic structure of the big band musicals of the 1930s and gave it a much

harder edge. Fully a decade before *Guys and Dolls*, it proved that the American musical could deal with a cynical, brainy, seedy underclass as well as the bland upper-class white tie and tails of what had gone before. That original stage cast in 1940, led by Kelly and Vivienne Segal was an amazing collection of unknowns on their way to stardom. June Havoc, sister of the Gypsy Rose Lee (their mother later to be immortalized in Sondheim's *Gypsy*), played the wonderfully named showgirl, Glady Bumps. Two other members of that cast, Robert Mulligan and a sixteen-year old Stanley Donen, were to become triumphant film stars, and Van Johnson was in there somewhere too.

It was Kelly, of course, who was the first to be grabbed by Hollywood. 'A unique, glib-footed tap-dancer,' wrote John Martin, 'who can turn dance routines into an integral element of the plot, has a feeling for comment and content that gives his dancing personal distinction.'

For MGM, Arthur Freed was on to him at once, although it turned out to be David Selznick who eventually made Kelly the better offer of $750 a week and no screen test. The problem was that Selznick had no film to offer, and instead sold him on to MGM. There, it was Judy who got him his first major movie role. She had seen him dance on Broadway and was so impressed that she convinced Freed to co-star him above the title in her next picture, *For Me and My Gal*, and Gene was never to forget his debt to her.

'Without Judy,' he said later, 'my first few weeks at MGM would have been even more miserable than in fact they were. At that time, I was constantly being thrown by the piecemeal way in which pictures were being made. I knew nothing about playing to the camera and I didn't even know whether I was being shot close, medium or long, or about the intricate business of hitting all the marks laid out on the studio floor for the movements of the actors. It was Judy who pulled me through. She was very kind and helpful, more helpful than even she realized, because I used to watch her to find out what I had to do. Judy was only just nineteen but she had been in pictures for six years. I was amazed at her skill; she knew every mark and every move. All I could do for her then was to help with her dancing. She wasn't really a dancer but she could pick up a step instantly, and as a singer she was incredible – she only had to hear a melody once and it was locked in her mind. I learned a great deal about making movies doing *For Me and My Gal* and much of it was due to Garland.'

The story of *For Me and My Gal* again cast Kelly as a heel, this time a singer and hoofer who deliberately crushes his own fingers in a cabin trunk to avoid being called up to fight in the First World War. His rival for Judy's affections (she was also playing a vaudevillian) is the infinitely more decent George Murphy, who does not take kindly to the arrival of the new boy in town. 'When I was offered *For Me and My Gal*,' recalled Murphy,

LEFT *Judy at home in Beverly Hills with her first husband, David Rose.* ☆

BELOW *Gene Kelly proudly
exhibiting his draft-dodging
injury to Judy in* For Me and My
Gal *(1942).* ☆

"Don't you understand, Jo? I did it for us—to get us our big chance!"

BELOW *Director Norman Taurog working with Judy on set.* ☆

'Freed told me that it was to be a vehicle reuniting Judy and me from the previous year's *Little Nellie Kelly*. But as soon as we began shooting, MGM decided to get behind Kelly and I was rapidly demoted to third lead. Interestingly, the studio later got hundreds of letters complaining that Judy should have gone off with me at the close instead of that heel Kelly.'

Nevertheless, critics were generally more enthusiastic about this one than, amazingly, they had been about *The Wizard of Oz*: 'Miss Garland,' wrote the *New York Herald Tribune*, 'is now someone to reckon with; she is a saucy little singer and dances passably. The songs are good, the story maudlin, but then again, that's the history of vaudeville. Judy looks thin and frail throughout the picture but she seems to have developed enormously as an actress and entertainer since her last screen assignment … she is already well graduated from a sort of female Mickey Rooney into one of the more reliable song-pluggers in the business. She also begins to show symptoms of dramatic sensitivity, discipline and talent. Of all the youngsters who have graduated on screen into mature roles in recent years, she has the surest command of her especial brand of make-believe.' The film itself now looks both sentimental and naïve, but, shot in the immediate aftermath of Pearl Harbor, it contains some of Busby Berkeley's most intimate musical work, without his usual overkill of dance numbers and with an unusual number of close-ups.

Judy was still nineteen when shooting started. This was already her fifteenth film and the first one in which she was permitted to have two leading men, either of whom could plausibly have taken her to bed. She had, and not before time, escaped the puppy love if not always the puppy fat.

Privately, too, her life was getting more interesting. With her husband already out of sight and out of mind fighting in the war, Judy began to date a considerable number of her film and radio co-stars. Few of these lasted beyond a few dates and many, such as the young Rock Hudson and Van Johnson (not to mention her old friend Roger Edens), were gay. With all of these she felt especially safe.

The affair with Tyrone Power had broken up his marriage, but there were now even more intriguing rumours around the lot about Judy's sexual adventures. She'd started a lesbian affair with the singer/songwriter Kay Thompson, and, as Axel Madsen was later to note in his *The Sewing Circle*, 'Judy was to sustain a bi-sexual life from now onwards, albeit one understandably closeted in secrecy until well after her death.'

In retrospect, her attraction to women and gay men (who in her maturity would always be her most loyal fans) is understandable. For much of her childhood she had lived in a female-dominated household, surrounded by a strong mother Ethel and two sisters. The men who drifted in and out of the house – and indeed her early professional life –

were, in her view, either a waste of space or, like her stepfather, actively hostile. Her friendships, with some notable exceptions, were throughout her life to separate sex from relationships, and her later marriages reflected these twin attractions to both homosexuals and sexy if sometimes brutal men.

But Judy was now also driven more and more into fantasy. On the verge of her twenties, she had already spent most of her teenage years being other people rather than living her own life, and it was therefore hardly surprising that she could very seldom tell where reality left off and the movie in her mind took over. Gene Kelly was just one example of this. Happily married to Betsy Blair just before they arrived in Hollywood, he had no sexual interest in Judy whatsoever, but this did not stop her imagining, and even sometimes believing in, an affair with him.

She was, however, considerably sharper and more focused when it came to her career, and she now knew that if she was to escape the fate of Shirley Temple or Deanna Durbin, she had also to establish herself very quickly in straight dramatic roles.

Yet MGM were never keen to let her get too far away from the stereotype they had already invented for her. Her next picture, *Presenting Lily Mars*, was in this respect, a perfect compromise, in that although once again Garland was cast as a stagestruck, small-town girl who gets lucky on Broadway with the Tommy Dorsey Orchestra, the plot was based on a melodramatic novel by Booth

RIGHT "Usually when you have a great voice you are not a good actress – or, when you are a good actress you don't have a great voice. Judy has everything in the world." (Producer Joe Pasternak) ☆

Tarkington which allowed her to do rather more acting than she ever had with Mickey Rooney.

The producer, Joe Pasternak, later remembered: 'Everybody in her audience always felt that Judy was singing to them individually and that was her great trick. She was now so convincing on the screen that everybody thought she was acting for them. She was not too glamorous for the women to dislike or be jealous of her, and she was beautiful enough that men fell in love with her. On the screen she sold herself to everybody, both individually and collectively.'

As soon as *Presenting Lily Mars* was in the can, however, Metro sent Judy straight back into the arms of Mickey Rooney. Like Judy, he was now deeply emotionally unstable and constantly changing partners while condemned, like her, to go on playing more or less the same role on-screen. This time, for *Girl Crazy*, he was to play a college boy sent into the Wild West, where Judy and he stage a spectacular Western jubilee, and if that plot sounds vaguely familiar it was, of course, this Gershwin score which, suitably augmented and with a new book, became early in the 1990s the long-running West End and Broadway hit, *Crazy For You*.

Even in its original Broadway and Hollywood form, *Girl Crazy* had one of the best scores Judy was ever to sing. 'Embraceable You', 'But Not For Me', 'Bidin' My Time' and 'I Got Rhythm' all started here, as did the first serious reports of Judy's studio

LEFT *Judy Garland hits all the right notes in* Thousands Cheer. ☆

RIGHT *Doing the show right here: Judy biding her time in* Girl Crazy. ☆

breakdowns. Busby Berkeley was originally assigned to direct what would have been his fourth film with Garland and Rooney. However, by now drinking heavily and devastated by a road accident in which he had inadvertently killed a pedestrian, Berkeley had enough troubles of his own, and only a few weeks into the shooting of *Girl Crazy* he and Judy came to a temperamental parting of the ways. The picture was closed down for a month, Berkeley was replaced by an infinitely safer pair of hands, those of Norman Taurog, and only a few traces of Berkeley (notably the 'I Got Rhythm' section) were to make it to the final cut.

Sixty years later, it is difficult to assign precise blame to the Berkeley/Garland bust-up, and it may well have been that on this occasion Buzz was as much if not more at fault than Judy. Unfortunately for her, it was on *Girl Crazy* that all the reports of her on-set tantrums and delays began, and very soon they were to become axiomatic. In fact, it was not Judy who insisted on Buzz being replaced but the producer, Arthur Freed, who saw in these two explosive and unstable characters a combination which would no longer serve his unit or their movies and therefore stepped in to solve a very real personality clash.

Shooting was certainly not helped by a freak sandstorm on the barren stretch of desert just outside Palm Springs where *Girl Crazy* was on location. But even during the month-long shutdown for the change of director, Judy was not allowed to stay idly at home. Instead, she was forced to return to *Presenting Lily Mars* for some retakes and was then to spend the next few weeks, once *Girl Crazy* had resumed under Taurog, frantically shuttling from one picture to the other.

Although *Girl Crazy* did superbly at the box-office, and Mickey and Judy were to make three more musicals together, they were never again to be paired as a couple. There was now a feeling that it was all over. Indeed, their next vehicle, *Babes in Hollywood*, was abandoned even before the script reached a final draft. Clearly they were now somewhat ancient to play innocent teenagers defying their parents and doing yet another show 'right here in the barn'.

James Agee, for *The Nation*, could find nothing to recommend *Girl Crazy*, 'unless you are curious to see how they made one of the biggest box-office successes of the year out of very little…Miss Garland, like Rooney, is a good if strident vaudeville actress with a kind of straightness and sweetness which might lead her on to straight dramatic roles.' As for one of the greatest scores ever written by the Gershwins, Agee did not even notice it.

Early in 1943, with the war now approaching its height, Judy began to do troop concerts all over the United States. Indeed, she had been the first Hollywood star to play to the troops, within days of Pearl Harbor, and found in these concerts one form of escape from Metro as well as wonderful practice for the stage career she was to forge after the war.

RIGHT *Having a well earned meal on the set of* Meet Me In St Louis *(1944).* ☆

Privately, though, she was an emotional mess, and it was at this time that her sister Virginia suggested that she could do a lot worse than start seeing a psychiatrist. Judy agreed, and signed up with Dr Ernst Simmel, an elderly and distinguished German refugee. She was to get on and off the couch regularly for the rest of her life. Not surprisingly, neither her mother nor 'Uncle' Louis was especially keen. A psychiatrist on the scene would mean that their power over Judy now had to be shared with a third party. From Judy's point of view it just meant reeling from mother through studio to psychiatrist, desperately trying to find out, without much success, who she really was and why she seemed to have been unhappy for her entire life to date.

Her studio now began to announce project after project for Judy, which somehow never got made. For a while she was slated for the first remake of *Showboat*, but when this did emerge, fully ten years later, the role of Magnolia went to Kathryn Grayson. There was also an intriguing plan to film the life of the great French cabaret star Gaby Delys, but that also fell apart at an early stage. At the time, it was not unusual for studios to make banner announcements of movies which, for a variety of reasons – unavailability of actors, terrible scripts, director problems – never came to fruition.

In the event, Judy's next film was to be a guest-starring appearance in *Thousands Cheer*, one of the starriest and most successful of all wartime omnibus musicals. The cast also included, in separate

LEFT *On the set of* Meet Me in St Louis *with the director she was about to marry, Vincente Minnelli.* ☆

BELOW *Sisters in St Louis – Margaret O'Brien, perhaps her only real child-star successor.* ☆

sequences, Mickey Rooney, Lucille Ball, Lena Horne and many others. Around the central storyline of Private Gene Kelly romancing Colonel's daughter Kathryn Grayson, Judy simply sang one number, 'The Joint is Really Jumping', which introduced José Iturbi, already a well-known classical conductor, as pianist in his first Hollywood film.

Off the screen, Judy was now embarked on the longest-lasting of her lesbian affairs and, to make matters still more complicated, it was with her own personal publicist, Betty Asher, another highly disturbed lady and one who was a few years later to take her own life. It was also widely thought that Betty had only recently been the cause of Lana Turner's divorce from Artie Shaw.

To add to the complexity of her current situation, Judy was now dating an amiable actor called Tom Drake, with whom she was shortly to star in one of her greatest musicals, the one that was to bring her together with her second husband, Vincente Minnelli. *Meet Me in St Louis* was based on some *New Yorker* magazine memoirs by Sally Benson. It had only two very slender plotlines – one concerning Judy's crush on the boy next door (Tom Drake), and the other about her family's horror when their father considers moving to New York just before the opening of the World's Fair in St Louis, the Universal Exposition of 1904.

This was the film that made the reputation of its director, recently promoted from his dual roles as Broadway set designer and Hollywood scriptwriter.

His name was Vincente Minnelli, he was just thirty-four years old and he was, like Judy, the child of a touring vaudeville family who had spent most of his early life on the road. He had already directed the all-black musical *Cabin in the Sky*, and a comic vehicle for Red Skelton, but it was on *Meet Me in St Louis* that his immaculate taste and impeccable sense of period style really flourished. As it turned out, one of his greatest talents was for handling and shaping the most difficult of stars, and was a particularly deft hand when it came to working with Garland. She had been initially reluctant to trust herself to a relative newcomer, but the early friction between Judy and Vincente soon turned into yet another Garland obsession with the wrong man. For although she soon became determined to marry him, it was already by no means a secret that most of Minnelli's romantic interests were focused on men.

In this atmosphere of considerable sexual and professional tension, Judy began yet another of what were to be her near-lifelong habits, arriving for work at least two hours late. It was Mary Astor, playing her mother, who snapped first, '"Judy", I asked her, "what the hell's happened to you? You were once a trouper. You now keep the entire company out there waiting two hours for you to favor us with your presence. You know we're stuck, there's nothing we can do without you in most of these scenes." Judy grabbed me by the hand and her face crumpled up. "I just don't sleep, Mom," was all she said.'

Nevertheless, *Meet Me in St Louis* turned out to be a triumph for all concerned. Ralph Blane and Hugh Martin wrote Judy at least three songs that she would continue to sing until the very end of her life: 'The Boy Next Door', 'The Trolley Song' and 'Have Yourself a Merry Little Christmas', which did fine once they deleted the original second line that ran, 'It may be your last'.

By the time shooting ended, Minnelli had succumbed to Judy's need for him, and moved into her new home in West Hollywood. Her mother remained violently opposed to yet another man who might take her bread-winning girl out of her clutches, but Garland was now set on having more than just an affair with Minnelli. Marriage was what she wanted, and for that she would have to divorce David Rose, still away fighting in the war.

One of the many reasons for the triumph of *Meet Me in St Louis*, quite apart from a brilliantly dark Halloween sequence, was that Minnelli insisted on bringing with him to the film at least two of the talents with whom he had started on Broadway. Irene Sharaff came up with superlative period costumes, and Lemuel Ayres, who had just designed the original Broadway *Oklahoma!*, now came out West and built, on the back lot at Metro, the fully-finished house in which for the sake of realism and continuity, Minnelli wanted to shoot the picture, instead of the more usual movie-set house with plywood walls and no third dimension.

It was, even in its own terms, a fine movie, but the chord it struck in its audiences could perhaps only have happened in time of war. The family in *Meet Me in St Louis* represented the best of what Americans wanted to believe about themselves. While their husbands, sons and fathers were fighting on foreign soil, they needed to know what they were fighting for; and the values of small-town warmth, innocent love, neighbourliness, family closeness and civic pride made up the goals of most Americans of the time. *Meet Me in St Louis* reminded them of who they were or, at any rate, of who they mostly wanted to be.

Despite a difficult shoot, with not only Judy but also Joan Carroll and little Margaret O'Brien succumbing to a variety of real and imagined illnesses, *Meet Me in St Louis* still came in roughly on budget and only a week or so late and eventually went on to become the greatest money-maker of its time after *Gone with the Wind*. It also put Judy at number ten in the list of top Hollywood box-office earners.

MGM renewed Garland's contract for another five years at $5,000 per week, a considerable improvement on her previous earnings but still in no way comparable to the kind of money they were paying such male stars as Mickey Rooney and Clark Gable.

Judy's next picture was *The Clock*, a wartime drama about a young couple who, like millions of others at that time, only just get together before he has to go away to war, possibly never to return.

LEFT *Under* The Clock *(1945) with co-star Robert Walker.* ☆

Judy's husband was played by Robert Walker, who worked with her again a year later in *Till the Clouds Roll By* before going on to star for Hitchcock in *Strangers on a Train*, but then to die all too young in 1951.

The original director of *The Clock* (based on a story by Paul and Pauline Gallico) was to have been Fred Zinnemann, a young Austrian who had only recently graduated from short-subject documentaries. Three weeks into the shooting, an already familiar pattern repeated itself and not for the last time when, as on *Girl Crazy*, Judy and her director came to a parting of the ways in what are usually called 'artistic differences'. Judy retired hurt for three weeks and when she returned to the set, the new director, to the surprise of nobody very much, was the man she wanted to marry, Vincente Minnelli. It is a measure of her financial importance to the studio that this still very young woman was in a position of sufficient power to bring about this kind of reassignment, a privilege which at that time was only accorded to a movie's producer or the studio head.

Once again, though, it is important to recall that, contrary to popular legend, Judy was by no means the only cause of the film's problems. Robert Walker was also an emotional wreck, drinking heavily to overcome the recent collapse of his marriage to Jennifer Jones. When shooting was finally over, Judy had reached an unusual state for her. She was happy. 'Darling,' she wrote to Minnelli, sending him an exquisite desk clock, 'whenever you look at this to see what time it is, I hope you will remember *our* Clock. You knew how much this picture meant to me and only you could have given me the confidence I so badly needed. If the picture is a success (and I think it's a cinch) you, my darling Vincente, will have been responsible for the whole goddamned thing. Thank you for everything, my angel. If only I could say what is in my heart – but that is impossible so I'll just say God bless you and I love you.'

LEFT *With Mickey Rooney, Busby Berkeley and producer Arthur Freed at the Hollywood Canteen.* ☆

6. Zing Zing Zing

1945 — 1950

The Clock was to gross a respectable $2 million in 1945, but that compared very unfavourably with the Garland musicals, which were averaging around $12 million, and as a result Judy was not given another straight dramatic role until *Judgment at Nuremberg* in 1960. Between the two, she made eight more musicals.

'After the war Judy was slim and talented but strung as tight as a violin string'

Helen Rose

RIGHT *A pistol-packing Harvey Girl for the film of that title (1946).* ☆

Meanwhile, early in 1945, on the usual promotional tour for *The Clock*, Judy returned for the first time in several years to New York. Her director and lover, Vincente Minnelli, was of course with her, and it was with him that she began to discover the delights of Broadway. Far from Culver City and the ever-watchful eyes of her mother and 'Uncle' Louis, Judy now fell happily into a whole other show-business community, one made up of theatrical singers and dancers and actors with whom, she now realized, she really had much more in common than with the more plastic of her MGM contemporaries. Although only on stage for a few minutes to introduce her picture, she rediscovered the joys of a live audience, half forgotten since her vaudeville childhood, and vowed there and then that this would ultimately become her favourite showbiz environment. She wanted to come back, and come back she soon would.

Back in California, however, this was just another of her many problems. Not only was she short, inclined to change from chubby to emaciated, and already with the reputation for being trouble on the set, but she also now began to be considered almost too theatrical for the camera. Years of playing stagestruck girls who become stage stars had distanced her from the naturalistic camera techniques which were just beginning to be fashionable. Actors who had been stage-trained like Judy were being supplanted by a whole new generation who knew nothing but the camera. The

vast majority of Judy's musical numbers had been set on some kind of stage, and it was rapidly becoming apparent that she was now far better in longshot across the footlights than in the more intimate close-ups which audiences were coming to demand. At this moment of the coming of television, Judy at twenty-three already seemed old-fashioned – a creature of vaudeville and radio rather than the new post-war world.

Her next movie was another attempt to recapture the period-musical audience who had flocked in such numbers to *Meet Me in St Louis*. *The Harvey Girls* was set in the Wild West of the 1890s, and concerned a group of travelling waitresses. Originally, the MGM dream factory had meant it as a non-musical for Lana Turner, but the only trace of that original script was the somewhat vague idea of rivalry between the 'nice' young waitresses and the older, wiser, saloon girls.

Two future musical stars, Angela Lansbury and Cyd Charisse, were to be found further down the cast list, but *The Harvey Girls* was really celebrating the end of the Second World War and a brief return to the Good Old Days of showgirls, period sets and costumes, lilting tunes and wonderful dancing. The fact that all of this was propping up a remarkably feeble storyline fortunately went unnoticed, despite the fact that at least eight writers, including an uncredited Guy Bolton (P.G. Wodehouse's legendary partner of the 1920s Jerome Kern musicals), had toiled to very little avail. Judy's old team of Arthur

LEFT *Judy between bridegroom Vincente Minnelli and "Uncle" Louis B. Mayer at her second wedding.* ☆

Freed and Roger Edens were now co-producers, and the director was the same George Sidney who had been behind the camera at her very first screen test almost exactly ten years earlier.

Because of her top ten box-office status, Judy was in a strong position at MGM, strong enough to be able to insist on having other old friends around her on the set. Thus Kay Thompson did the vocal arrangements with Ralph Blane, and Garland brought in Helen Rose, who had last seen her in vaudeville, as her costume designer, together with Gene Kelly's mentor, Robert Alton, as choreographer.

It was Helen Rose (no relation to Judy's soon to be ex-husband) who, seeing her for the first time in almost fifteen years, was struck by the change in Garland. 'She was now slim and talented but strung as tight as a violin – quite different from the happy little roly-poly I had first seen on stage singing her heart out.'

Not everyone took a genial view of Judy's emotional troubles: 'Sure,' wrote Anita Loos, the witty inventor of Lorelei Lee in *Gentlemen Prefer Blondes*, 'Judy's mental attitude may have been pathetic, and we all felt kind of sorry for her, but, Jesus, was she boring about herself.'

It was during the shooting of *The Harvey Girls* that on 15 June 1945, after a quiet divorce from a newly returned David Rose, Judy married her second husband, Vincente Minnelli. She was just twenty-three and he was more than ten years older.

Her dislike of her stepfather made her ask the other shark in her life, old 'Uncle' Louis B. Mayer, to give her away, and Vincente's best man was her old friend, Ira Gershwin, whose lyrics for *A Star is Born* would give Judy her last great screen triumph only nine years later.

Whether or not at the time of their wedding Judy knew what was already common knowledge around the studios and restaurants of Culver City, that Minnelli had always been very gay indeed, has been a matter for conjecture ever since. But certainly they were very much in love, so in love that Judy agreed, for the first time in her life, to take a year off in the hope of having his baby.

The Harvey Girls had been a long and difficult picture to shoot, but once again the problem was not only Judy's occasional physical and mental breakdowns. Things got worse when her co-star Ray Bolger was badly scalded by a burst of steam from the train carrying the waitresses through the picturesque scenery of the Wild West and, to add to this chapter of accidents, another leading actor, John Hodiak, was hit by a blazing beam during a fight scene. Nor was George Sidney's directorial life made any easier by the fact that since The Harvey Girls was a real life and still-functioning waitress service in the West, representatives of the organization were constantly on the set to keep a sharp eye on the representation of their name and reputation.

No sooner was *The Harvey Girls* safely in the can than the new Mr and Mrs Minnelli took off for an

LEFT *Judy on the set of the all-star* Ziegfeld Follies *(1946) with cameraman George Folsey (left) and electrician Al Fenton (right).* ☆

extended honeymoon at a Sutton Place apartment in the New York that had already become their spiritual home. One night, walking by the East River, Judy gave Vincente perhaps the best wedding present she possibly could; impulsively she opened her handbag and threw into the water several bottles of the upper and downer pills which had been for many years her daily diet. Things were definitely looking up, and by the time they returned to Hollywood towards the end of 1945 they were able to announce another happy event: Judy was pregnant.

As usual, however, it wasn't quite as easy as all that. She had committed to her next big musical, *Till The Clouds Roll By*, a heavily romanticized but authorized account of the life and work of Jerome Kern. Sadly, Kern himself was to die suddenly not long after the movie went into production, causing a revaluation of the entire project. As a result, what had been designed as a linear biography now became a collage of Kern songs, thereby allowing Judy to film all her material out of sequence before her pregnancy became too apparent.

Judy was cast as the Broadway star Marilyn Miller, who had introduced many of Kern's best songs. Minnelli agreed to stage and direct her numbers, although the overall Freed production was directed by Richard Whorf, but the result of separating Judy's sequences and shooting them in advance of the rest of the picture was that her Marilyn Miller went from being a central figure in the plot to little more than a girl coming on to sing a few numbers. True, they were all classics, 'Look for the Silver Lining', 'Sunny' and 'Who Stole My Heart Away' and allowed Judy in what was now a comparatively minor role to keep her profile high in a film which also starred June Allyson, Kathryn Grayson, Lena Horne, Dinah Shore, Frank Sinatra, Van Johnson, Tony Martin, Gower Champion, Cyd Charisse and Angela Lansbury. Curiously, the one actress that the film tried to made into a star, Lucille Bremer, was seldom heard of again. As *Time Magazine* noted, 'The picture in fact is little more than a series of production numbers of Kern songs, but Judy Garland is charming as Marilyn Miller and still more charming when she sings "Who".'

With Liza now well on the way, it was to be almost another year before Judy was seriously ready to take on another picture; but she did in the meantime agree to do yet one more guest-star shot, this one in the *Ziegfeld Follies of 1946* in which, intriguingly, she did not sing a song but instead performed a satirical sketch. In 'The Great Lady Gives an Interview' she did a remarkable parody of Gertrude Lawrence in the original *Lady in the Dark*, a development of her teenage comic mimicry which had been all too seldom exploited in the intervening years.

Once that was in the can, Judy did nothing for the next six months but prepare for the arrival of her first child. This was her longest break from stage or screen since she was three years old, and although she was now off all the pills, she was still by no means either relaxed or happy in her new domestic life. As Minnelli himself later recalled, 'Her attempts to be a wife and future mother were not exactly triumphant; Judy's desire for constant and instant approval around the house was pathological. She would begin to clean the kitchen floor or do a needlepoint canvas only to abandon it to the servants after about ten minutes. Even so, I had to reassure her that it was the cleanest half of a kitchen floor or the greatest few stitches in needlepoint ever achieved by any human being.'

Their baby arrived (by Caesarian section) early on 12 March 1946 and was duly christened Liza May after Gershwin's song 'Liza' and Vincente's mother May. All too predictably, Judy now sank into post-natal depression from which she was not to emerge for several months. The problem was not just Liza. MGM had renegotiated her contract up to $5,600 a week and, perhaps more importantly, were now promising that she would only have to make two movies a year. But they also raised the penalties for failure to arrive on set. This could result in suspension, withholding of pay, and, as the ultimate deterrent, a total cancellation of her contract.

Typically, instead of celebrating the new terms, she began to panic about whether she could live up to them, especially as a new project was looming. This was to be *The Pirate*, which would reunite Judy with the now much more established Gene Kelly.

The script of *The Pirate* had a curious and contorted history. It had started out as a 1911 German stage comedy about a notorious pirate becoming the mayor of a respectable island in the Caribbean. In 1943, the Broadway playwright S.M. Behrman had turned it into one of Alfred Lunt and Lynn Fontanne's rare flops, building in a wandering actor who impersonates the pirate in order to win the hand of a young girl.

Vincente and Judy had seen the play in New York and decided that what it lacked was songs and dances. They persuaded Arthur Freed to commission Cole Porter to write an original score for what was to become their next project together. Shooting started just after St Valentine's Day in 1947, but on the second day gossip columnist Hedda Hopper found Judy in her dressing-room, 'shaking like an aspen leaf and in a frenzy of hysteria, claiming that all who loved her had now turned against her and were tapping her telephone calls.'

One of the many writers on *The Pirate*, the perennial Anita Loos, later wrote: 'I recall an early day at the studio when mild little Vincente Minnelli was waiting to direct Judy in one of the big scenes. As usual, she was late for work, and everybody, including Kelly, Gladys Cooper, and 150 extras, had been marking time since eight in the morning. Finally, at noon, Vincente was summoned to the phone to learn that Judy required him to get home at once and escort her to an ice-cream parlor for a soda.'

BELOW *Proud parents: Mr & Mrs Minnelli on the set with their baby Liza.* ☆

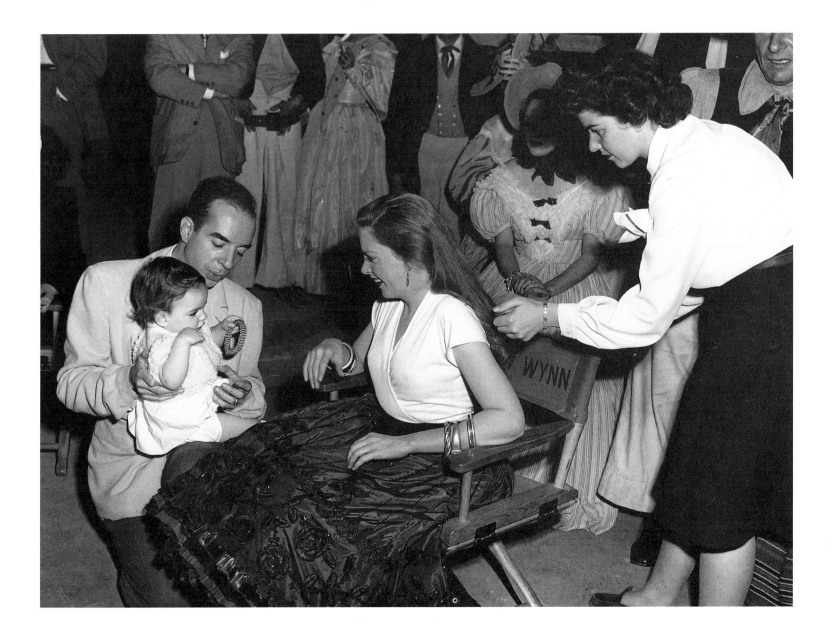

Not entirely surprisingly, the Minnelli marriage was already coming apart at the seams. Vincente may well have seemed a mild little man on the set, but he was passionately committed to professionalism, and the fact that his own wife now seemed intent on destroying his own movie was more than he could stand. With all Judy's problems, by June the film was only half finished but already nearly a million dollars over budget. When they finally reached Kelly's 'Pirate Ballet' in August, the movie had taken 135 days to shoot, for ninety-nine of which Judy had been absent.

But the Garland magic was still intact on-screen and she and Gene transcended a movie which had started out as a parody of the swashbuckling films of Douglas Fairbanks Sr, only for its makers to discover that in those days before television re-runs, nobody under about sixty had ever seen a Fairbanks picture.

The Pirate is well outside the mainstream of Garland musicals. It was the most strenuous and sophisticated movie that either she or Gene had ever attempted. It required virtuoso acting, dervish dancing and the mastery of a volatile, lusty Cole Porter score of which the highlight was, of course, the knockabout 'Be a Clown'.

The plot, even in the original German, was Byzantine, and by the time it had been rewritten by Behrman for Broadway, and then Joe Mankiewicz, Anita Loos and Joseph Thau for the movie, it was incomprehensible. Yet another rewrite took place when after shooting had started the husband-and-wife team of Albert Hackett and Frances Goodrich were brought in to clarify the dialogue. However, as they had always specialized in Nelson Eddy musicals, the style was again eccentric.

Of Judy's old team, Robert Alton was now choreographing with Gene Kelly; Kay Thompson and Roger Edens were again on vocal arrangements, and Lena Horne's husband, bandleader Lenny Hayton, was again the musical director.

LEFT *Judy with Gene Kelly as* The Pirate *(1948).* ☆

ABOVE *A poster for*
The Wizard of Oz. ☆

RIGHT *Judy with Toto.* ☆

BELOW *Ray Bolger,*
Bert Lahr, Judy and
Jack Haley off on the
Yellow Brick Road. ☆

PREVIOUS PAGE
Judy in possibly her
most famous role.

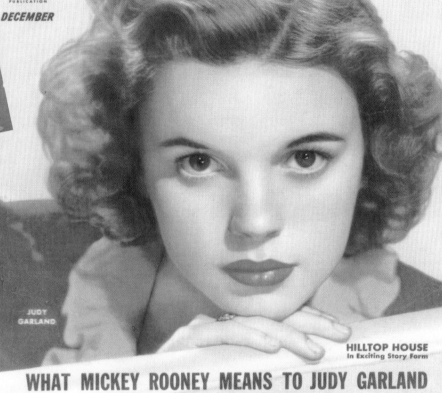

TOP LEFT *Lobby card for* Strike Up the Band. ☆

BOTTOM LEFT *Judy with Mickey Rooney in* Strike Up the Band. ☆

ABOVE *Judy as Mickey's perennial girl next door.* ☆

ABOVE *Judy in the 'Get Happy' sequence from* Summer Stock. ☆

RIGHT *Judy with Fred Astaire as the 'Swells' in* Easter Parade. ☆

WARNER BROS. PRESENT

JUDY GARLAND
JAMES MASON

We believe there hasn't been before, even once, such performances by motion picture stars, such perfection in motion picture entertainment!

'A Star is Born'

TECHNICOLOR AND CINEMASCOPE

SONGS BY
HAROLD ARLEN
AND
IRA GERSHWIN

'THE MAN THAT GOT AWAY'
'IT'S A NEW WORLD'
'GOTTA HAVE ME GO WITH YOU'
'HERE'S WHAT I'M HERE FOR'
'SOMEONE AT LAST'
'LOSE THAT LONG FACE'

JACK CARSON · CHARLES BICKFORD WITH TOM NOONAN · MOSS HART A TRANSCONA ENTERPRISES PROD · SIDNEY LUFT · GEORGE CUKOR · WARNER BROS.

54 453

ABOVE 'The best film ever made about life behind the cameras, lights, wind machines and cocktail bars of Hollywood' Dilys Powell, Sunday Times ☆

MAIN PIC The Rat Pack go to work: Dean, Judy and Frank on US television in 1960. ☆

TOP RIGHT Judy in The Pirate. ☆

BOTTOM RIGHT Judy in I Could Go on Singing; even though she didn't. ☆

OVERLEAF *Judy, as photographed by Douglas Kirkland.* ☆

BELOW *Laugh, Clown, Laugh .... Judy and Gene in* The Pirate. ☆

Another highlight of the film was Kelly dancing with the innovative and amazingly athletic Nicholas Brothers who are, at this moment of writing, fortunately still with us. Then they were two young black tap-dancers whose precise and elegant style was copied and studied by much older and more experienced performers. Although they were much younger than Kelly, he admired them enormously and had always wanted to work with them. *The Pirate* was his chance, and he spent every moment they were working watching them on the set. But even this was trouble, as the sight of a white man teamed up with black dancers cost the film several lucrative bookings in Southern states, even as late as 1948.

From first to last, *The Pirate* was to take almost a year to shoot and that included no less than two sanitorium stays for Judy. All the same, she was now only below Ingrid Bergman and Bette Davis in the female popularity charts and Metro was still prepared to tolerate a certain amount of her troubles. What's more, virtually everyone on the set and in the offices of MGM was convinced they were dealing with a huge hit.

Only Cole Porter, with his more cynical alert awareness of what audiences wanted in these post-war years, had his doubts and when the film was released, early in 1948, it was old king Cole who had, as usual, got it right, as Gene Kelly remembered: 'After the early previews, Vincente and I still believed we were being so dazzlingly

LEFT *Judy and Gene in a publicity still for* The Pirate. ☆

brilliant and clever that everybody would fall at our feet and swoon away in delight and ecstasy as they kissed each of our toes in appreciation for this wondrous new musical that we had given them. Boy, did we get that wrong. About five and a half people seemed to get the gist of what we had set out to do, and in retrospect you really couldn't blame any of the others. We just did not pull it off. Not completely. Whatever I did just looked like fake Barrymore and phony Fairbanks. That was the result of the damned elusive camera, which I had been trying so hard to tame. It all looked just wonderful in rehearsal. The sophisticates grasped it, but the film died in the hinterlands. It was done tongue in cheek, and I should have realized that parody and satire never really work on-screen. But I still thought Judy, for all her ever-increasing troubles, was superb, and what Minnelli did with color and design in that film is just as fine as anything that Hollywood has ever done.'

But the last word should go to the greatest American film critic writing at the time of its initial release, James Agee, who wrote: '*The Pirate* has the death's head culture-cute mirthful grin of your average Shakespearean comic and is ultimately about as unfunny. As an all-out try at artful movie-making, this is among the most interesting pictures of the year. Unhappily, most of the very considerable artistry that Kelly has put into this production collides head-on with artiness or is spoiled by simple miscalculation.'

In cash terms, *The Pirate* returned a respectable profit on MGM's investment. On a total cost of $2.5 million, the first release gross was well over $6 million, but in the light of the hostile reviews, Metro decided that the sooner Judy and Gene could be persuaded to return to less experimental material, the better for all.

The problem was that Judy was now not fit to return to anything. She had twice been hospitalized on the advice of her psychiatrist in private clinics, although at least there she did manage to find a few kindred spirits: 'I met some of the most charming people in Clinic, sensible, intelligent and humorous. As far as I could gather, not one of them was demented in the common sense. Most of us were just too highly strung and too sensitive for reality.'

7. Easter Parade to Summer Stock

1947 — 1950

By the time Judy got back from her last clinic stay, Liza was almost two. Despite the revised MGM contract, Garland was (as she would be for the rest of her life) badly strapped for cash. Still supporting her mother and several other relatives and staff on her studio payroll, and with no sense of how to control her expenditure or run a household efficiently, she somehow never managed to get into profit and, as always, decided that her one way out of the crisis would be to get back to work.

'I was a nervous wreck, jumpy and irritable from too little sleep and too many drugs. I just couldn't take the studio tension'

RIGHT *A Couple of Swells
... Judy with Fred Astaire
in* Easter Parade *(1948).* ☆

OVERLEAF *Peter Lawford
and Fred Astaire fighting
for the Easter charms of
Judy Garland.* ☆

The studio had decided to reunite Garland and
Kelly on a new Irving Berlin musical, *Easter Parade*.
But this too seemed jinxed from the outset. Just as
they were about to go into production, Gene broke
an ankle playing football in his back yard and the
only possible replacement, Fred Astaire, had to be
gently coaxed out of a premature retirement.

Worse was to come. The marriage of the
Minnellis, troubled from the beginning, was now in
such bad shape that Judy demanded her husband's
firing from *Easter Parade*; three weeks into the
shooting he was duly replaced by the rather less
inventive Charles Walters, a former hoofer who
had become a dance director at MGM. Not that he
was to have an easy time with Judy either. As he
wrote later, 'Judy loved to growl, and as soon as she
heard I was the new director on *Easter Parade* she
sent for me to say, "Look, sweetie, I'm no June
Allyson, so don't get cute with me. I don't bat the
eyelids or fluff the hair, buddy, I'm Judy Garland
and just you watch it."'

Irving Berlin also got short shrift when, at a
recording session, he tried to tell Judy how to phrase
one of his songs. 'Listen, buster', she hissed, 'you
write 'em and I'll sing 'em any way I like.'

But one good thing was to emerge from *Easter
Parade*. Once the studio had teamed her with the
rather more old-fashioned Fred Astaire, she realized
that she had in one sense come home. Intellectually
impressed as she had always been by both Minnelli
and Kelly, she now feared that they were trying to

push her down a road she could not travel. She knew what she could do best, and what she could do best was always going to be traditional rather than experimental.

As for Fred: 'I loved to work with Judy … she was a super talent … great sense of humor … she wasn't basically a dancer, but she could dance … If she felt like it, she could do anything she liked on screen and learn it very fast … But that was on the good days.'

Easter Parade was essentially an update of Bernard Shaw's *Pygmalion*, also of course to serve as the basis for *My Fair Lady* some fifteen years later. The original screenplay was by Frances Goodrich and Albert Hackett, but among the many script rewriters was the future bestselling novelist, Sidney Sheldon. In all the versions, Judy was yet again a chorus girl who gets taken up by Astaire and turned into a star, while the score, a mix of old and new Irving Berlin songs, did not have a single dud, all the way from 'A Fella with an Umbrella' (Judy with Peter Lawford) through the tramp number 'A Couple of Swells', to the title song itself, or rather the song that, while actually called 'Happy Easter', is the one containing the crucial phrase.

But Judy's state of health was beginning to show, at least to those members of the press who were alert to it. Reviewing *Easter Parade*, an unusually perceptive *New York Times* critic noted, 'Judy, wan and frail, needs a little more flesh on her bones to give her more verve and bring her up to her old standard as an entertainer.'

As usual, the gossip columnist Louella Parsons was still tougher: 'Judy now has serious health problems and has been in and out of clinics all year long; rumors are that the Minnellis are close to break-up.' Even Liza couldn't add the necessary stability to their home life because, although she was thrilled with her daughter, Judy already saw her as a kind of threat, or at least a rival for the stage-centre position that she herself needed to occupy. As Liza herself wrote later, 'Millions of people adored my mother and they never even met her. Sometimes I felt just the same way myself.'*

Once again the MGM solution was to throw Garland into yet another movie in the forlorn hope that somehow a shooting schedule could cure both her depression and her paranoia. The picture they chose, which was supposed to reunite her with Fred Astaire, was *The Barkleys of Broadway*, from an original screenplay by Betty Comden and Adolph Green, which cast Judy and Fred as a latter-day Broadway musical comedy team threatened with separation when Judy decides to go for the higher art of straight dramatic theatre.

On this one, she never even got as far as the studio floor, as Oscar Levant recalled: 'I was looking forward to working with Judy but she never once appeared on the set. Arthur Freed and Louis B. Mayer both went to her Hollywood hilltop home but apparently no one, not even they, could persuade her to start the film. Finally, Ginger Rogers was hired to take Judy's place opposite her old

dancing partner and the picture got under way at last. Then, suddenly, after we had been shooting for about a week, Judy appeared on the set looking totally manic. When she poised herself behind the camera it was really too unnerving, not least for Ginger, and the director, Chuck Walters, finally asked her to leave. Judy refused, so Chuck took her by the arm and led her out, still shouting obscenities about Ginger.'

For days afterwards, Judy was unable to leave her bed. Her weight dropped to eighty pounds and she was fed glucose intravenously. Once again, old 'Uncle' Louis came to the rescue. Although his studio was now withholding $100,000 of Garland's salary for the chaos she had caused on *The Barkleys of Broadway*, leaving Judy and Vincente in yet another cash crisis, Mayer was prepared to do a deal. If she would sing just one song in the new Rodgers and Hart musical biography *Words and Music*, he would pay her $50,000 for just a couple of weeks' work. All she would really have to do for that sizeable cheque was to get her ass out of bed and down to Culver City.

This she managed, singing 'I Wish I Were In Love Again' as her last ever screen duet with Mickey Rooney, and it turned out so successfully that a few weeks later Mayer asked her to return to the set for another $50,000 to sing 'Johnny One Note'. There was now just one little problem with this request: her success in the first number had restored at least some of her confidence and, as a result, she gained at least thirty pounds in weight. In the movie, therefore, she sings her first number looking like a refugee from a prison camp, and her second looking like Kate Smith.

It was now becoming clear in the Garland household that the poisonous Louella Parsons had been right about the collapse of the Minnelli marriage. Vincente, for his own self-preservation, was more than ready to call it quits: 'My own self-assurance was now at its lowest ebb. A treadmill was transporting us to disaster, and we had to run double-time in the opposite direction just to keep stationary. Judy had already tried to kill herself at least once by ramming a broken glass into her neck, and we were forever trying to keep the truth about her out of the papers and, more importantly, away from MGM, not to mention our daughter who, mercifully, had a wonderful old-fashioned nanny to keep Liza out of the firing line on the battlefield that was now our marriage. I'd obviously failed Judy, and those periods in her life when she was least able to cope with the world coincided with the years of our marriage. It was an indictment I could not ignore. But Judy had failed me too. She would never be able nor willing to create a home with me. Our future would always be marred by her self-indulgence and compulsion. I had either humored them or fought them for years, and the events had been so cataclysmic that when we were not throwing things at each other, we clung together just for survival.'

The Minnelli marriage was not to reach a formal divorce for two more years, but it was effectively all over by the time she began to work on her next picture, *In the Good Old Summertime*. Heartbroken at being parted from his beloved little daughter, Vincente nonetheless moved out of Judy's house and she went back to work on a picture for which she had not been the original casting.

June Allyson had been slated to star opposite Van Johnson in this musical remake of the old 1940 Margaret Sullavan/James Stewart hit *The Shop around the Corner*, which was of course to become the source of an altogether different Broadway and London stage musical, *She Loves Me*, and which itself was an adaptation of the Hungarian romance by Ferenc Molnar about two quarrelsome colleagues who find they have inadvertently fallen in love by mail. Its latest reworking is indeed the 1999 movie *You've Got Mail*, which sets romance on the Internet.

When it became clear that June Allyson's current pregnancy would make the plot a little difficult to believe, Judy was brought in at very short notice and, because she didn't have long to obsess about this one, it worked out very well indeed. As its producer Joe Pasternak commented, 'When Judy was on form she could just look at the script once, learn it, and never flub a line. The same was true of her musical routines. Very seldom did you ever have to make two takes with her. She would just watch a stand-in going through the paces once and then just do it. She hardly ever looked at her own

RIGHT *Judy and Mickey in* Words and Music *(1948), wishing they were in love again.* ☆

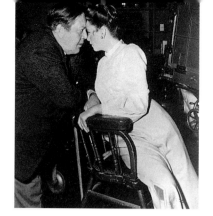

daily rushes, and when she did, she always became convinced that she would never work again – her self-confidence really was always that low.'

In the Good Old Summertime was relocated from Budapest to Chicago and it was a musical of considerable, if quiet charm. The score, however, was totally unoriginal and forgettable and of the songs Judy sang, only the old hit 'I Don't Care' and the relatively new 'Meet Me Tonight In Dreamland' were to prove of any use to Judy in her later concert life.

Judy never seemed happy with the film, and her on-screen romance with Van Johnson, an actor she had never much liked anyway, was a lot less convincing than the secondary love plot involving the veteran S.Z. 'Cuddles' Sakall and Spring Byington. Indeed, one of the best reasons nowadays for watching the movie at all on television is to catch the fleeting screen debut of Liza Minnelli, aged two and a half, on the closing credits.

If everything had gone according to plan, which with Judy it never did, her next film would have been considerably better. A couple of years before, MGM had bought the rights to Irving Berlin's stage hit *Annie Get Your Gun* which he had written for Ethel Merman. But Merman had never really made it as a movie star (her personality was too large and theatrical to sit right on the more intimate cinema screen), and the gun-toting Annie Oakley seemed a natural for Garland instead.

Now that it was about to go into production, the first of several major problems arose: Metro insisted that Busby Berkeley should direct, despite the fact that he and Judy had not spoken since she effectively had him fired from *Girl Crazy* six years earlier. Judy was also very far from the top of her form – still popping pills and deeply insecure about her professional and private future. They began as always with the music, laying down voice and music tracks and shooting the production numbers well ahead of the plot.

But within only the first few days, producer Arthur Freed was already worried enough to call in someone he knew to be a 'safe pair of hands', the director Charles Walters, for some advice. 'My God, it was just horrible.' remembered Walters. 'Judy was at her absolute worst. She couldn't decide whether to be Ethel Merman, Mary Martin, Martha Raye, or just herself. Berkeley was no better. He had no concept of what the picture was all about and was shooting the whole thing like a stage play. Everyone would come out of the wings, say their lines and then back away upstage for their exits.'

Freed immediately fired Berkeley yet again, and handed the movie over to Walters. Even so, they could not save the Garland situation. One glimpse of her rushes, throughout the screening of which she stuffed Benzedrine pills into her mouth, was more than enough. She walked straight off the lot, checked herself back into a clinic that very afternoon and never returned to the set. Technically, therefore, despite almost all other printed accounts, she was

ABOVE *Judy eye to eye with director Robert Z. Leonard on the set of* In the Good Old Summertime *(1949).* ☆

RIGHT *The one that got away: Judy in costume tests for* Annie Get Your Gun *before she was replaced by Betty Hutton.* ☆

not in fact fired from *Annie Get Your Gun*, but in terms of her career prospects and studio reputation she might just as well have been. Now that she was back in the clinic, MGM put her on suspension anyway. They had spent an unprecedented $700,000 buying *Annie* for her and a further half a million on pre-production. By the time they could recast it with the altogether more reliable Betty Hutton, Judy's star had well and truly dropped out of the MGM firmament. Even now, knowing what we have subsequently learnt about Judy, Berkeley, the pills and the booze and the professional hysteria surrounding the shooting of *Annie Get Your Gun*, the newly rediscovered footage of Judy singing 'Doin' What Comes Naturally' shows her well able to transcend all the problems and disasters. She still shines, her charm is, at least on-screen, intact, and her contact, through the camera lens, directly to the audience is still undiminished.

After a few weeks in the clinic, where she underwent a course of electro-shock therapy, Judy returned home to become the mother from Hell. Alone in the house with only Liza and her servants for company, she began sending the three-year-old around the circuit of Beverly Hills birthday parties, often inviting herself to stay in order to exhort her little girl to sing louder and kick higher when the kids were dancing.

Back at MGM, her prospects of any kind of future were not exactly enhanced when old 'Uncle' Louis himself, who had been her most fervent supporter

RIGHT *Judy taking exercise on the set of* Summer Stock *(1950) supervised by director Charles Walters.* ☆

for more than ten years, found himself at the heart
of boardroom battles which would soon result in his
loss of absolute power and eventual enforced
retirement. Nevertheless, there were at least two
men on the lot who still believed absolutely in Judy's
talent. One of these was Charles Walters, who had
reluctantly seen her depart from his *Annie Get Your
Gun*, while the other was Gene Kelly who felt that
he owed her his training in movie musicals. So, at
the very end of 1949, the two men approached her
with producer Joe Pasternak and the suggestion of
another project.

Judy badly needed to get back on the MGM
payroll; although the studio ultimately paid the
$50,000 in medical costs for her recent illness, she
was still in tax troubles and having to support
herself and Liza as a single parent household now
that Minnelli had left. Moreover, the new movie
Summer Stock was taking no chances. It was a
throwback to her early Mickey Rooney barn-dance
musicals in which she now played a struggling
Connecticut farmer who allows Gene Kelly to set up
a summer theatre in one of her barns.

The shooting took all of six months and twice
Judy tried to quit. In the end, however, she and
her director and co-star all struggled through, with
a doctor always on the set to check Judy's pill intake.
Two months after the shooting was finished, the
studio decided they had to have just one more
number for the finale – Judy returned and shot 'Get
Happy' in less than a week. The only problem was

that during the weeks when she thought the film was over, she had again managed to lose thirty pounds, so the Judy in 'Get Happy' looks like some quite different star who has just come in for the finale.

Despite the brilliance of that one closing number – Judy in her tilted fedora is the one sequence that many of us would choose if we could only have one Garland song – her self-confidence was again at such a low ebb that two months before the film opened she again tried to kill herself. On this occasion, Minnelli was actually at her house visiting Liza and according to several reports, he too made a suicide attempt. The inevitable press coverage was not exactly helpful, but it did at least encourage Judy and Vincente to go finally for their long-anticipated divorce.

Katharine Hepburn went round to give Judy a pep-talk next day. 'You're one of the three greatest talents in the world. Now your ass has hit the gutter, there's no place to go but up. So, goddamnit, go.' A somewhat wittier response to the unwanted publicity came from the music department at MGM: 'Dear Judy, So glad you cut your throat, all the other girl singers need this kind of break.'

As so often when she was in real trouble, Judy fled to New York, where she was thrilled to find herself getting mobbed outside several cinemas then showing *Summer Stock*. Already, the Broadway theatre community, still at that time light years away from Hollywood with very few crossovers, had taken Judy to their hearts as if they knew that sooner

or later she would end up back on stage for them, rather than suffering yet another humiliation and attendant suicide attempt back in sunny California.

On this occasion, however, she did return to Hollywood and even began to work again. The first offer was to replace June Allyson (pregnant yet again) on *Royal Wedding* opposite her beloved Fred Astaire. This time the director was to be Stanley Donen (Gene Kelly's co-choreographer and long-time directorial colleague), because her old friend Chuck Walters had asked to be taken off the picture once he knew that Judy was on board: 'I felt no animosity toward her, but I just couldn't face a repeat of the *Summer Stock* experience. Judy could not help herself when she was behaving badly, and when she was feeling good you would never have met anyone wittier, sharper, better company, and bright as a button. But those good days now were getting fewer and further between.'

But not long into the shoot, Judy walked off the lot yet again. Her replacement was Jane Powell, and now for Garland it really was all over. She was called one last time to the studio, in theory to start pre-production on *Showboat*, but as soon as the new studio boss, Dory Schary, saw her he realized that she was a liability: 'It just became too much to ask any of my producers or directors to work with her. She simply had to go and it broke my heart.'

Judy was never to work at MGM again. Her studio career had lasted just thirteen years during which time she had made thirty pictures.

LEFT *Judy and (standing) director George Cukor, with photographer George Heune celebrating the seventieth birthday of Ethel Barrymore in 1949.* ☆

8. Broadway Baby: Judy at the Palace

1951—1953

Garland's behaviour on the set of *Royal Wedding* may have been the final straw for MGM, but in a curious way it led to the rebirth of Judy herself and, some would say, her belated arrival at independence. The enforced retirement of old 'Uncle' Louis meant that Metro had abruptly ceased to be her family and became an impersonal, hard cash business instead. Dory Schary issued a statement clearing the studio of its apparent heartlessness: 'With the responsibility, and in justice to other artists, the studio had only one recourse, which was to take Miss Garland out of the picture and suspend her contract. We assumed whatever losses were involved, recast it [with Jane Powell] and went ahead. The substitution of any artist in any picture is never made on an arbitrary basis, and certainly a person of Miss Garland's talent is not easily replaced. This replacement is not a hasty move, prompted by pique or irritation; it is the last resort arrived at with great regret after all other means have failed.'

> 'She's the greatest all-round performer living. She can break your heart one minute and leave you laughing the next' Gene Kelly

RIGHT *At the Barrymore birthday party, Judy, Billie Burke (centre) and Katharine Hepburn admiring a new portrait of Ethel.* ☆

Even Judy was able to find a kind of wry humour in her final departure: 'I had been suspended so many times that my feet virtually never touched the ground; but I was now a very tired girl and I think MGM realized that. They were very nice about releasing me from my contract – in the end it was fine of them and good for me. I felt like I had shed a whole suit of armor.'

His statement indicates that Schary was frightened of a backlash, and sure enough, it came with remarkable speed. On her own, faced with supporting herself and Liza on an income which had suddenly dried up, leaving her as always with no cash reserves, Judy again tried to take her own life. This time it was her neighbour, Katharine Hepburn and her old benefactor, Louis B. Mayer, who physically drove pressmen off her front porch. They sent for her mother, now living in Dallas with Judy's sister, Virginia, who had settled there and was running a cinema.

When Judy recovered, leaving Liza with her ever faithful nanny, she went to New York to celebrate the success *Summer Stock* and it was there, at the Capitol Theater on Broadway in September 1950, that she was first to hear the soon all too familiar shrieks of an obsessively protective live audience. Judy, they screamed, we love you, we understand, come back to us soon. Her dismissal from MGM and her latest suicide attempt had almost overnight turned her from studio star into victim, and it was that new status which was to provide the key to her

LEFT *Judy with her third husband, impresario Sid Luft.* ☆

later life career and to her rapport with the homosexual lobby which was from now on to support her as it had supported Dietrich, Piaf and all the other perceived victims of the fame game.

It was in New York at that time that Judy met the man who would become her third husband. Sid Luft was a showman and a survivor of the old school, much closer to Liz Taylor's Mike Todd than the gentle, poetic Vincente Minnelli. Luft had started out as a secretary to Eleanor Powell, gone into the used car business, joined the Royal Canadian Air Force, briefly become a test pilot, and then married the actress Lynn Bari, for whom after the war he produced a series of dire 'B' movies. His lifelong passion was the racecourse, but he had a kind of macho strength which appealed to Judy in her current state of weightlessness.

True, their relationship did not get off to a great start. Back in California, she and Sid were both charged with being drunk and disorderly after a minor car crash. The other driver sued Sid for $15,000 on account of broken teeth acquired not in the accident, but in the fight which ensued. Humphrey Bogart, not renowned for his quiet good taste and a hellraiser in his own right, reckoned that Luft 'lacked class' but there was no doubt that he was now what Judy most needed – a strong pair of hands to put her back together again, and haul her out of the near-bankruptcy to which back taxes, medical expenses, and the cost of running the Hollywood house for Liza had now reduced her.

It was Luft, together with Judy's New York agent, Abe Lastfogel, who now had the brainstorm which would relaunch her in front of an altogether new audience. Just after the war, the manager of the London Palladium, Val Parnell, had watched with amazement as Danny Kaye had broken all the house records of that most famous of all variety theatres. Ever since then, Parnell had been on the look-out for other Hollywood stars who could repeat the phenomenon. Since about 1948, he had issued a standing invitation for Judy to make her British stage debut, and his offer was now worth nearly $75,000 for a month's work. This, Luft and Lastfogel decided, would be the moment for Judy to take it and effectively get reborn on the other side of the Atlantic.

Typically, having signed the contract, Judy began to panic and threatened not to leave her house, let alone California. This time it was Fanny Brice, one of her neighbours, who was sent around to sort her out: 'You are going to London,' she told Judy, 'with the voice and the talent God gave you to make everybody here proud of you. Keep your head up, your eyes on tomorrow, and to hell with yesterday.'

Judy opened at the London Paladium on 9 April 1951. She had taken the precaution of hijacking both Roger Edens and Kay Thompson from her old studio gang to support her, and it was they who finally got her on-stage to face a packed house. It would not be true to say that all her overnight reviews were ecstatic – the British press gleefully reported that she was looking distinctly chubby compared with the waif-like Dorothy in *The Wizard of Oz* which was still, even after twelve years, their immediate touchstone for Garland. But it was the *Evening Standard* which suddenly understood the new pact that Judy had made with a live audience: 'It is not only with her voice but with her whole personality that she fills the theatre. She can command pathos without being maudlin and Garland is now vastly better than her material. This quality of vibrant sincerity opens up possibilities which probably she herself has failed to realize. Last night we saw a brave woman but, more than that, we saw a woman who has emerged from the shadows to find that her public likes her even more as what she is than as what she was.'

During her triumphant Palladium debut, in the solo concert which was to define the remaining eighteen years of her working life, Sid Luft was officially appointed her business manager, and now Judy had even acquired the courage to tackle the press on the perennial issue of her weight. 'It's quite simple,' she told *The Times*; 'fat I'm happy, and thin, I'm miserable.'

Back in California, Judy began to get her divorce from Minnelli and prepare for the marriage to Luft; now happily no longer tied to any studio schedule, she was able to return to the Palladium in June for a charity matinee fundraiser in aid of the family of one its greatest home-grown stars, Sid Field. She shared that bill with Laurence Olivier and Vivien

RIGHT *One of covers of the hundreds of albums that document Judy's music.* ☆

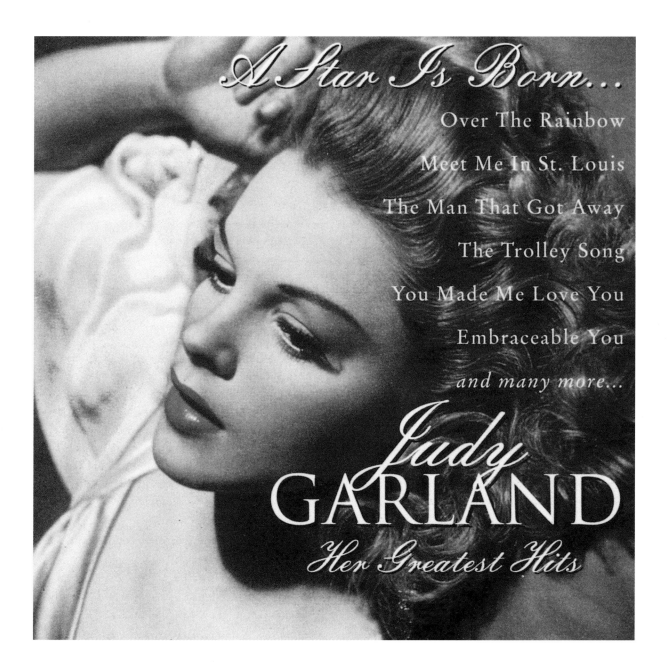

Leigh, Danny Kaye and Orson Welles, and Richard
Attenborough, who later noted that even in such
incredible stellar company it was only again Judy
who tore the place apart: 'No matter who was on-
stage, they looked as though they did not belong
there once Judy appeared. It wasn't just the songs
or the way she sang them; it had nothing to do with
pathos or memories; it was just sheer magic.'

On Broadway there were rumours that Judy
might go into *South Pacific* or one of the other
long-run hits of the period, but Luft now had a
much better idea: if Judy could triumph at the
London Palladium, then surely she could do the
same at the Palace? The old vaudeville theatre on
Broadway had fallen on hard times, but Luft
remembered two things: Judy's childhood start in
vaudeville itself, and the fact that many of her most
successful films had been about a girl in some sort
of emotional or financial trouble who, in the last reel,
suddenly reinvents herself as the stage star we
always knew she was about to become.

Even so, two shows a day for the whole of
October 1951 seemed rather ambitious, in relation
not only to Judy's still shaky emotional and physical
stability, but also, as there were 1,700 seats in the
Palace, to whether her audience was now really
sizeable enough to fill them twice daily. *Variety*
noted, 'If anyone can do it, this little bundle can',
but, as always now with Garland, there were those
in print and in private already gleefully forecasting
either her cancellation or a humiliating disaster if

she did take to the stage. It has to be noted that a considerable element of Judy's 'fan club' now consisted of people who turned up at her shows in the macabre hope that she wouldn't.

On this occasion at least, she was to disappoint the drama queens and the gloom merchants. This first season at the Palace, the first time she had ever appeared solo on-stage in front of an American theatre audience (the personal appearances and the troop concerts had nearly always been in the company of at least one other star, usually Rooney) was simply to repeat her Palladium triumph. All the same, the pressure of thirteen performances a week (there was no Monday matinee) and making the 'Judy at the Palace' LP, which was to be her best-seller, did lead to yet another collapse backstage. Vivian Blaine, on a rare night off from the original run of *Guys and Dolls*, was in the audience and finished the show for her. Judy went back into hospital but this time there was to be an unusually happy outcome. So triumphant had she been at the Palace that the management asked her to extend way into the New Year of 1952. In return, they would slash her performance schedule to a mere ten shows a week and ultimately eight. By the time she closed, at the end of February, she had broken all attendance figures at the Palace and had taken a total of $800,000 over nineteen weeks, a solo show record which was not to be beaten in New York for another thirty years.

At the end of the run Judy was given a special Tony award and a golden nameplate for the doors of the backstage dressing-room where she was so clearly now to make her home.

Judy and Sid returned to California and there she repeated the triumph in concert seasons both in San Francisco and Los Angeles, where Louis B. Mayer led her first standing ovation on home ground. But just as it began to look as though Judy could now spend most of her time on the road, another pregnancy intervened. Luckily she had now married Luft, and even he agreed that, given her precarious health, it would make sense to stay home until the new baby was born. This did not mean that she could not work at all; Bing Crosby was now running the most successful of all weekly radio shows and, with the illness of his beloved wife and co-star Dixie Lee, he turned to Judy to replace her. Over the next six months, Judy re-established her radio stardom until, in November, 1952, her second daughter and the first of her two Luft children, Lorna, was born.

LEFT *Judy at Churchill's in London with Bruce Brace in 1951.* ☆

9. A Star is Born

1954

By now, Judy and Sid had had plenty of time to consider Garland's future. Ironically, her stage success had suddenly made her desirable again for motion pictures, and this time it was Warner Brothers, not MGM, who came up with the best offer, a three-picture deal which would start (and, as it sadly turned out, conclude) with a remake of one of the home-grown stories that had always proved a Hollywood winner.

'This Is the story of my life and I hate every frame of it'

A Star is Born is a film that has been, for more than half a century, central to the mythology of the dream factory. First shot in 1932 as *What Price Hollywood?* with Constance Bennett and Lowell Sherman, and then again with Janet Gaynor and Fredric March in 1937 and, most recently and catastrophically, in 1976 with Barbra Streisand and Kris Kristofferson, its most famous and memorable version was the one that went into production in 1953. It did so against considerable opposition, not least from Judy's old mentor Arthur Freed who, when told that Garland had gone over to Warners for a big musical to be produced by Luft, memorably noted 'Those two alleycats will never make a picture.'

This was a widely held view around Hollywood at the time. Garland, despite her recent comeback, was still reckoned to be hopelessly unreliable, and Luft far too inexperienced for what was now to be a wide-screen musical of considerable length and ambition. Early in her MGM years, Judy had even done a brief radio version of *A Star is Born*, recognizing there and then that the story of a young actress marrying an established movie star, whose fame she first outgrows and eventually eclipses, would suit her very well indeed.

During pre-production in 1952, Judy's mother Ethel was found dead in a car-park; she had collapsed on her way to work at the aeroplane factory where, for several years, since Judy's own financial troubles, she had been making a living.

Their relationship had reached an all-time low a few months earlier when Ethel had tried to sue Judy for non-support and given an interview in which she had noted, 'Judy has been so selfish all her life that all she ever wanted to be was an actress, never my daughter. I hope the press will now forget me as surely as Judy has done.'

Torn by grief and guilt for the way that she had always blamed her mother for everything that went wrong in her life, Judy went into another nervous collapse from which she was only rescued by Luft's single-minded determination to get her into the studio on time for the start of *A Star is Born*.

With the relatively inexperienced Luft himself as producer, and George Cukor as director, the 1954 remake of *A Star is Born* went from its original budget of $4 million to a total of over $7 million. But this was not entirely Judy's fault; though the shooting was hamstrung as usual by her chronic unpunctuality and the days when she couldn't get herself on to the set at all, the main reason for the overspend was that quite early in the shooting the new wide-screen technique of CinemaScope was perfected and Cukor decided they had to go with it whatever the expense of the reshooting involved.

Additionally, this was Cukor's first musical and, amazingly, his first film in colour. As Judy said later, 'This picture had to be the greatest – I had too much at stake for it to fail.' But even the casting was to prove problematic. Precious few male stars wanted to take on the burden of working with the mercurial Garland, and of those that did, most were all too aware from the outset that this was going to be her picture and nobody else's, not least because the producer happened also to be her husband.

Laurence Olivier politely declined the role of Norman Maine; Richard Burton proved unavailable, Tyrone Power unaffordable and Cary Grant unwilling; other refusals came swiftly from the ailing Humphrey Bogart, Marlon Brando, James Stewart and Montgomery Clift. When the job finally fell into the lap of James Mason, it was at a time when he himself admitted that his Hollywood career was 'no longer getting anywhere very fast'.

But this was still to be an immensely classy project, not only because of Mason and Cukor but also thanks to a brilliant score by Harold Arlen and Ira Gershwin and a screenplay by one of America's most distinguished playwrights and stage directors, Moss Hart.

Once shooting started, as one bystander recalled, 'If you saw James and Judy together on that *A Star is Born* set, there was no doubt that Judy had fallen in love with him. She had slimmed down, done everything to make her performance work, and was just desperate to please him even though Luft was always hovering around to make sure the affair never got too serious. Judy was very often way out of control, and certainly Luft never really managed to calm her down, but James was always wonderful with her, very patient when she was late on the set, and was forever demanding close-ups of himself so Jack Warner, who was ultimately paying the

bills, wouldn't notice how badly she was delaying the production. Judy and James were just wonderful together, and his quiet professionalism seemed to make up for her unreliability – he kind of nursed her through it.'

Like Dirk Bogarde a decade later on her last film, Mason was the kind of quiet, poetic English actor who took pride in helping an obviously disturbed woman, though he did not get on nearly so well with Cukor. George wanted the part of Norman Maine to be played as a reflection of the life of the late John Barrymore, on whom the role of the declining, drunken star was always believed to have been originally based. James, however, wanted to go for something rather more personal and it was, in the end, a matter of letting him find the character for himself. In that last scene, where he breaks down and decides to commit suicide by simply swimming out to sea and therefore away from the studio which has been his ruin, Cukor just lets the camera stay on him for a very long time and all his feelings just come pouring out.

As for Mason: 'When I first arrived in Hollywood, I had put myself at a very great disadvantage, because I did not do any of the right things, so to be offered a picture like this was very special, even after it had been turned down by properly established people like Cary and Bogey. I had the greatest possible faith in Cukor and an admiration, a sort of love, for Judy, who was marvellous to work with. Of course, she had her difficulties; she'd got

into this strange way of life when she was a kid at MGM, where the top brass wanted to get the most out of her so they didn't take it amiss if she took a little pick-me-up in the morning and sleeping pills at night. It became a habit with her, and of course, in time got worse. On the set, she didn't put in as many hours as a less talented woman would have had to do, but she was wonderfully easy. Some mornings she couldn't start before eleven because of all the pills, but once she was awake, she was great – thoroughly professional and a joy to work with.'

One of the central problems of *A Star is Born* was always its length. Both Cukor and Garland, deeply in love with the Hollywood myth, indulged themselves in a picture of which one of the most brilliant reviews was later to come from Noël Coward in his diary: 'Whatever has happened to the once-famous Hollywood sense of timing? In spite of fine acting performances by Judy and James, and a lavish, highly over-coloured production, it drags interminably. Every song is attenuated to such a length that I thought I was going mad. One in particular, "Born in a Trunk", starts quite brilliantly but by the time it was over, and we had endured montage after montage and repetition after repetition, I found myself wishing that my darling enchanting Judy was at the bottom of the sea. The picture runs for three hours; cut down to two it might have been really exciting.'

And originally it was much longer than that. To Jack Warner's horror, the first answerprint came in

LEFT *'I am Mrs. Norman Maine'; Judy with James Mason in her last classic* A Star is Born *(1954).* ☆

ABOVE *A star is drunk –*
Mason interrupting
Garland's Oscar
acceptance speech in A
Star Is Born. ☆

at four hours and a vast commercial problem immediately became evident to all. Even at three hours, the all-important picture-palace managers across the United States could only squeeze in two showings a day instead of the four or five then customary for normal-length movies. Exceptions had indeed been made, most recently for *Julius Caesar*, but whereas that was reckoned to have a limited release anyway, *A Star is Born* was meant to be the major money-making musical of the year.

With both Cukor and Judy refusing to get it anywhere below three hours, Warners did a hatchet job of their own and got it down just below that crucial watershed. Many good scenes and musical numbers were lost in the process and not fully restored to the print until 1983.

The movie premiered early in 1954 at the Pantages Theater in Los Angeles. It was the starriest and biggest that Hollywood had ever organized and one of the first to be televised live coast to coast. Interviewed as part of the telecast, the Hollywood gossip columnist Hedda Hopper gushed at the enormous crowds outside the cinema, 'Isn't this just show business? Five years ago Judy was replaced on *Annie Get Your Gun* by Betty Hutton. Yesterday Betty Hutton announced she was giving up movies. And look at Judy now. Isn't that just wonderful?'

James and Judy were both in the running for Best Actor and Actress Oscars, and for Judy it turned into a black comedy all its own. On the night of the 1954 Oscar ceremony Judy was back in hospital, not this time for another nervous breakdown but for the birth of her third and last child, Joey Luft.

Television had just begun to interest itself in carrying the Oscars live, and so strongly was it believed in the industry that Judy would win that a camera crew was set up by her hospital bed several days in advance, in order to broadcast her delighted reaction live to the nation.

An entire scaffolding gantry was built outside her hospital window to house the then cumbersome television cameras while sound recordists carrying lengthy boom microphones kept crashing into all the doctors, nurses and friends who were trying to celebrate the safe arrival of Judy's first son.

As the announcement of the Best Actress award drew closer, nurses around Judy's bed were co-opted into holding lights and cables, and an elaborate cueing system was devised whereby someone down the corridor would watch the live transmission and then cue Judy in at the moment of her triumph. There was just one little snag – she didn't win. The Best Actress Oscar that year went to Grace Kelly for *The Country Girl*, and even as she approached the podium the television crew without a word started to dismantle all their equipment and disappear from the hospital, leaving several exhausted nurses to try to return it to normal life.

To add insult to injury, Mason too lost out, in his case to Marlon Brando who won for *On The Waterfront*. The picture was nominated for Oscars in six categories, but humiliatingly beaten in all of them. There were many who believed, with Groucho Marx, that the denial of major Oscars to *A Star is Born* amounted to 'the greatest robbery since Brink's', and conspiracy theorists soon became convinced that Hollywood was just determined not to let Judy back into the studio heartland. Not only was she still unreliable but she had committed the still greater offence of going back to live performance outside of Los Angeles. In truth, the oft-remade *A Star is Born* has always had a problem at awards ceremonies precisely because it is a lethally effective storyline, suggesting (as surely as any of the equally disillusioned screenplays of Clifford Odets) that Hollywood is no place to build a life, a career, or even a marriage.

But while Warners announced that they had 'over-relied' on their star, critics around the world began to write Judy the best reviews of her entire working life. *Time Magazine* called *A Star is Born* 'just about the finest one-woman show in modern movie history', while for the British *Sight and Sound* Penelope Houston perceptively added, 'The special fascination of Garland's acting is the way it somehow contrives to bypass technique; her control is a little less than complete but her

emotion therefore comes through as it is, utterly neat. In this incandescent performance Garland seems to be playing entirely on her nerves; she cannot therefore fail to strike at ours.'

As for the reviewer in the *Spectator*: 'Garland has lost a little in looks, but gained enormously in talent. Warm, sensitive and touching she always was, but now her pathos has a poignancy and her singing a passion. After hearing her "The Man That Got Away" and "Born in a Trunk", I felt she had seized from my hand the torch I carry for her and scorched my soul with it.'

Garland was not to make another film for six years, and her last three were in no way as starry or notable. *A Star is Born* was therefore effectively her farewell to the Hollywood movies in which she had lived out virtually the whole of her career, and to the world to which she had given her first thirty-two

LEFT *'One of the grandest heartbreak dramas to have drenched the screen in years' (New York Times): James and Judy on the beach where he is eventually to drown himself in* A Star is Born. ☆

years. From now on, she was to be back on the road where she had started as a child, singing a gradually declining series of solo concerts and ultimately losing the battle for any sustained stage or screen comeback.

All the same, many more successful and secure actresses would have given their eye teeth to end up in a film like *A Star is Born*. In the almost forty years since it was first released, the film has acquired an afterlife very nearly as potent as that of *The Wizard of Oz*, with which Garland first achieved stardom; and those of her fans who did not wish her to be forever going over the rainbow found in *A Star is Born* yet another metaphor for her uneasy life, even if, on this occasion, the real-life Garland role of the drunken defeated has-been was actually played out on-screen by James Mason.

But because, on its first release early in 1954, *A Star is Born* did disappointingly, not least due to the scheduling problem caused by its unusual length, any plans that Jack Warner may have had to keep Judy to their original three-picture contract were immediately abandoned. Judy was now faced with supporting a husband and three children with no visible means of making a living beyond a record contract which did not even begin to pay the bills.

RIGHT *Judy and little Liza on the set of* A Star is Born. ☆

10. Back From The Brink

1955 — 1969

The Luft marriage, never good, was now very shaky indeed. 'From the very beginning,' she told a friend later, 'Sid and I were never happy. I don't know why, I really don't. For me it was work, work, work, and I never saw much of Sid as he was always dashing off to line up my next concert. I wasn't made any happier looking in mirrors, seeing myself balloon up and down.'

'It's so lonely by myself. Good Night'

RIGHT *Judy at her most overweight, greeting Frank Sinatra after a 1955 concert.* ☆

Both Judy and Sid were chronically unfaithful to each other but, just as Liz Taylor found herself time and again drawn back to Mike Todd, so Judy would return to Luft, not only because he was the father of her two younger children but also because now, with neither her mother nor 'Uncle' Louis to turn to in a crisis, Sid was really all she had, the only one with any real interest in her career or her future since they were, of course, his meal ticket too.

Realizing that Judy was now too unreliable for a sustained concert tour, and that Hollywood had no interest in her at all after the financial disappointment of *A Star is Born*, Sid now turned to the only medium they had not yet explored, commercial television. Since she had always thrived on radio, it seemed logical to move her across to its replacement in the home as soon as possible, and in September 1955, Judy therefore made her first television special, the CBS *Ford Star Jubilee* on which she sang 'For Me and My Gal' and 'A Couple of Swells' with David Wayne.

The show was watched live by twenty-five million Americans, more than had ever seen her on any stage, and this first programme established overnight a whole new future career. Judy was also now making occasional Las Vegas concert appearances and it was there, that summer, that she and Sid had the dubious distinction of co-inventing the Rat Pack, of which the most famous and consistent members were Frank Sinatra, Dean Martin, Sammy Davis Jr and Peter Lawford, with all of whom Luft was now a regular drinking companion. Judy herself was more often into the pills than the booze, and would carry around with her an entire pharmacopoeia of Seconal, Dexedrine, Benzedrine, and all kinds of other drugs of which she seldom read the labels and almost never followed the directions for use.

Her debts were now up to around $300,000 and not helped by a summons to appear in a New York court, charged with having never paid any taxes on her triumphant Palace season. On this occasion, the judge even made her hand over to the court most of her jewellery and clothing.

In desperation, by her own admission 'fat and ugly' she returned to the Palace in September 1956, when the comic Jerry Lewis brilliantly summarized her stage appeal: 'People now know all the troubles that Judy has been through. And who among us isn't plagued with troubles too? So people with all kinds of worries and problems and heartaches go see her and they identify with her. When she sings, she is communicating for them all the emotions they can't communicate themselves because they don't have a stage or a microphone or talent. Stout women in the audience identify with her and the people who remember their own unhappy childhoods also identify with her. All the people whose insides have been torn out by misery identify with her, and she sings for all of them. She sings with a thousand voices.'

Sometimes, though, her audiences would not just look ugly, they would turn ugly, especially when she was playing nightclubs unprotected by the gap of an orchestra pit. On New Year's Eve 1958 she was back at Vegas doing a gig at the Flamingo when two drunk women climbed on to her little stage screaming, 'You're fat and you can't sing a note – get outta here.' On the other hand, in this same year, Garland played sell-out concerts first at the Chicago and San Francisco opera houses and then at the Metropolitan in New York.

By now she was desperate to get out of the Luft marriage, but as he was her only manager this was clearly going to be a difficult manouvre. For his part, Sid, equally depressed by the marriage, was nevertheless devoted to his two small children and determined if only for their sake to keep holding Garland together. When *A Star is Born* was first released, Judy was still just thirty-two. As one of her many biographers, Chrisopher Finch, has noted, 'Some days she would look fifteen years older than that, and most days she would behave as though she were fifteen years younger.'

Solemnly named 'First Vice President' of the Rat Pack (Lauren Bacall was voted 'Den Mother', Sid Luft 'Cage Master' and Humphrey Bogart 'The Rat in Charge of Publicity', with only David Niven denied office on the grounds that he was English), Judy now spent night after night drinking with the boys and trying to separate Bogey from her husband when they got into one of their many brawls. These usually started with Bogey telling Luft that he would never be a class act: 'You can't buy it and you don't

acquire it like a suntan; I can tell you, my friend, that you have never had class and never will. I know all about these things because I was born with class and I've learned to live without it. Now scram, my friend, and take that boring little wife with you.'

Whether at Ira and Lee Gershwin's or any of these Rat Pack gatherings, Judy was nearly always asked to sing and would give impromptu solo concerts which nobody who was there on the good nights ever forgot. Her problem, as in her stage work, was simply one of timing; because singing was her only real escape from an increasingly awful reality, she just never knew when to stop and could frequently be found at four in the morning singing to the departing backs of the very last guests to leave the party.

The years of the Luft marriage in these late 1950s were hallmarked by brawls, nervous collapses, occasional breathtaking concert triumphs and, as her elder daughter Liza was later to recall, frequent escapes from hotels down the service elevator in the small hours to avoid paying the bill. The saddest thing about these moonlit flights was, as Liza also remembers, that on the way out of the back door her mother would always say solemnly to the frightened little girl, 'Now remember, your mother is Judy Garland. It will all turn out all right in the end.'

Sometimes of course it did. But too often the phoney suicide bids, the inability to stay sober for long and the impossibility of reaching the stage at all some nights, meant that she was losing her grip even over her own children. After Judy's death, Liza returned to Minnelli and Lorna to Luft with a new-found adult admiration for what their fathers had put up with at the shaky hands of their mother.

If all else failed – and by the beginning of 1959 it had – there was always the chance that European audiences could still be won over to the extent of a standing ovation, and from now on it was to be in London that Judy would regularly try to put back the increasingly tacky pieces of her ramshackle career into some kind of coherent whole.

That autumn, like many other Hollywood stars, she campaigned for the young John F. Kennedy, and for a while it seemed that with the start of the new Camelot Presidency, Judy, like America itself, might be up for a make-over. She even got herself a couple of new agents, Freddie Fields and David Begelman, who began the tortuous process of unscrambling her affairs from those of Sid Luft.

In 1961 her new managers put her back on the road, playing often one- or two-night stands in towns and theatres as far down the touring scale as some of those in which she had started as a Gumm Sister little more than twenty years earlier. This particular tour, however, climaxed at Carnegie Hall with one of her last great one-night stands, as *Life* magazine reported: 'Judy is back to the very top of her form, singing far better than recently at the Palace or the Met. She is not only the most electrifying entertainer

RIGHT *Trim again, and back to being a hoofer: Judy rehearsing with Dean Martin and Frank Sinatra for a 1962 television concert.* ☆

to watch on-stage since Al Jolson, but she has moved beyond talent and beyond fame to become the rarest phenomenon in all show business. Part bluebird and part phoenix rising from her own ashes, she is now a legend in her own time.'

Early in 1962 she returned to California to do a one-off *Judy Garland Show* for CBS television co-starring Dean Martin and Frank Sinatra. Its success was such that Begelman and Fields were soon able to line her up for an entire series. But before that, she went briefly back to the movies, first to voice-over a feature-length cartoon called *Gay Purr-ee* about cats in Paris and then, more seriously, to play the role which won Judy her last Oscar nomination. This was as the pathetic German *Hausfrau* torn between achieving some kind of private happiness and seeking justice in *Judgment at Nuremberg*, for which she took sixth billing behind Spencer Tracy, Burt Lancaster, Richard Widmark, Marlene Dietrich and Montgomery Clift.

At this time, in a brief but not very memorable resurgence of her movie career, she also turned up in a dire André and Dory Previn musical called *Pepe* to sing one song and again for Stanley Kramer in a sombre piece called *A Child is Waiting* with Burt Lancaster, about the need to give retarded children a musical education.

But these movies were all now secondary to her concert life which lurched around from concert hall to nightclub and coast to coast without ever really finding its focus until, in June 1963, CBS

commissioned a television series scheduled to run through the 1963–4 season. At least two entire books (*Rainbow's End* by Coyne Sanders and *The Other Side of the Rainbow* by Mel Tormé) have been written about the making and unmaking of this series, which itself could serve as a microcosm of Judy's entire life and career.

Altogether, twenty-six hour-long episodes were not only commissioned but also made, if only just. 'My year on television,' said Garland later, 'was very enlightening, very funny, and either instant disaster or instant success. It went that way every week, one way or the other, but I did at least prove that I was reliable. They said I could never answer the bell for the second round but I turned out twenty-six shows and some of them were damned good.'

Some were, and some weren't. Although the series got off to a flying start by reuniting Garland with Mickey Rooney, and although it showcased a young Barbra Streisand and an even younger Liza Minnelli, some of the shows were just plain embarrassing – as Sybil Thorndike once said of audiences, some nights magic and some nights porridge. In truth, although there were all the usual Garland crises during which she would hide at home or in her trailer, because the show was recorded live she did have to appear once a week however drugged or under-rehearsed she was. And the problems were once again, contrary to popular belief, not entirely of her making. CBS had dis-

LEFT *Judy with Richard Widmark (left) in* Judgement At Nuremberg *(1961).* ☆

covered very early in the series that Judy's audience rating was never going to beat that of the *Bonanza* series they had scheduled her against, so they rapidly became disenchanted with the project, even though it had at least another five months to run.

Budgets were slashed and rehearsal time was cut; Mel Tormé gave up the musical direction once he realized that Judy was not in fact going to allow him the solo spots he had been promised; and despite a still amazing roster of guest stars (among them Tony Bennett, Ethel Merman, Lena Horne, Peggy Lee, Vic Damone and Donald O'Connor), the series soon plunged into an abyss from which neither it nor Judy ever quite recovered.

And yet, the whirligig of time does eventually bring in its revenges. Late in the 1990s, Garland addicts and other showbiz nostalgics began to realize that in the thirty intervening years there had never been another series quite like this one – so grainy, so dramatic and, above all, so demonstrably live that you could always be sure of something going wrong.

Videos made from poor quality black-and-white film transfers began selling in specialist showbiz shops; new fans and old admirers alike rediscovered a series which for all its technical and other faults was, in a curious way, historic, never more so than in the show which went out the week of the Kennedy assassination. Then, in sharp contrast to the sentimental media excesses going on elsewhere, Judy came out in a plain black dress and just, very softly, sang 'The Battle Hymn of the Republic' in what has to be considered one of the most moving moments in all television history. Nevertheless, CBS declined to continue with Judy's television series after the first commission was completed. What had started out as one of the richest deals ever done for television ($24 million if Judy had lasted four years) finished in complete meltdown, with Judy unable even to make the last episode, which became a ragbag of clips from the previous shows. During its twenty-six-part lifetime, the *Judy Garland Show* had gone through fifteen writers, three musical directors, three executive producers and two directors.

And that, effectively, was almost that. Judy went on working and living for five more years, made one more film and two more brief marriages, but she never again recaptured that moment of magic.

Not everything, however, was a complete disaster. As the television series closed, she received news that her most recent LP, 'Judy at Carnegie Hall', had won an unprecedented five Grammy awards. Judy, on the pills again, was finalizing her divorce from Sid Luft and she gave her two younger children a choice. Liza was already enrolled at the High School for the Performing Arts in New York, but Judy told Lorna and Joey that her only hope of making any money for them now lay in one-night concert performances all over the country. They could choose either to become the kind of backstage kids that she and her sisters had been, or to stay in the relative comfort and safety of California with a

BELOW *The penultimate film;*
A CHILD IS WAITING (1962). ☆

BELOW *On the set of her last movie, made at Shepperton Studios, near London,* I Could Go On Singing *(1962).* ☆

good housekeeper, and Mother would return with cash whenever possible.

Not surprisingly, given their heritage, the kids chose the road, and from now on, Judy and her two Luft children would criss-cross the country like refugees from Stephen Sondheim's *Gypsy*, forever trying to stay one step ahead of hotel bills or tax demands, neither of which Judy ever had the faintest hope of settling.

Even in her darkest hours, Judy could always count on an especially warm welcome from London audiences, and it was to the Palladium that she would return time and again to restore her rapidly crumbling career. On one of these London engagements she had made friends with the actor Dirk Bogarde, who, like so many of those close to Judy towards the end of her life, found himself rapidly being turned into a mixture of psychiatrist and male nurse.

Staying with Dirk one weekend in his country house, Judy brought him an original screenplay (by Robert Dozier and Mayo Simon) which told the story, rather less than coincidentally, of an American singing star visiting London to top the bill at the Palladium, who meets up with her first love. He is now a distinguished British surgeon who has then to get her through nervous breakdowns and alcoholic fits on to the stage where, alone, she finds her only real happiness. Clearly, this was intended to be some kind of closet biography of Garland, although she had once told Dirk that she herself was

The album that sold a million copies worldwide. ☆

never happy on-stage until the curtain came down at the end of the performance.

As Dirk was later to recall, 'Working with a concert performer like Garland was never going to be easy. She was fit for tying every day of her life with terror before the show, and the only moment that she felt good was at the end. Rewriting the script, I used a line she gave me. "You know when the light hits you they always say the pain and the fear go away but that's a goddamned lie. It never does."'

Dirk has always been convinced that Hollywood has been the death of some of the screen's most important talent: 'Take someone as magical as Marilyn; she was totally and utterly murdered by the studio system and, to a degree, so was Judy, whom I knew well and closely for about ten years. They killed Judy just as surely as they have killed anybody of any sensitivity. People tell me how brave I was to be in a film with Garland. I wasn't brave and I wasn't self-sacrificing. I also wrote all her scenes, and one of the greatest privileges of my acting life was to work with that actress. She was a monster, monstrous, but she was magic.'

Dirk, well aware of the script's limitations, but believing that it might still prove his beloved Judy's last chance at a movie comeback, added a brilliant scene pinpointing, through her character, her own wayward nature: 'You think you can make me sing? You can get me there, but can you make me sing? I sing for myself, I sing what I want to, whenever and wherever I want to – but just for me. I sing for my own pleasure. I'll do whatever I damned well want. Do you understand that?'

Once shooting started on *I Could Go on Singing* (originally and rather better entitled *The Lonely Stage*) there were all the usual Garland drink and drug problems. She behaved appallingly on the set, some days failing to show up at all, and wasting most of her now limited energy trying to get the director, Ronald Neame, fired.

Dirk, by contrast, behaved immaculately throughout, not only turning in the most self-effacing of performances but begging, bullying, nursing and cajoling Garland through every scene. Sadly, he was contracted to start another picture in seven weeks' time and once he left the set she fell to pieces yet again, leaving Neame alone to try to put together both his star and his movie.

The film opened on both sides of the Atlantic to respectful reviews and no box-office business of any kind. Although Garland fans would still queue around the block, both at the Palladium in London and Radio City in New York, to see their idol live, or maybe just to share in the macabre pleasure of witnessing her collapse on-stage, they were clearly no longer interested in seeing her in the comparative safety of a movie. Garland could have gone on singing, but on celluloid there wasn't much point. Which is rather sad because, thanks largely to Dirk Bogarde, *I Could Go on Singing* contains a truthful picture of Judy and her tortured life.

Although Judy was to be announced for two more movies, her appearance in *Harlow* (1965) did not get beyond the discussion stage, and though two years later she did agree to appear in the movie of Jacqueline Susann's *Valley of the Dolls*, she refused to leave her dressing-room on the first day of shooting. The days when such behaviour was indulged by MGM were long over, and Judy was promptly sacked, only to be replaced by Susan Hayward.

Garland herself was now struggling to get by on the concert circuit around the world. Asked how she was managing to survive at all, she once told a journalist in London, 'What do I do when I'm down? I put on my lipstick, see that my stockings are straight, and go out there and sing "Over The Rainbow".'

Film critics seemed to sense that they were never going to see her on the screen again, and the reviews for *I Could Go on Singing* at least in Britain amounted to premature obituaries. As Dilys Powell wrote for the *Sunday Times*, 'Watching Judy Garland I have a surge of affection.... It is for something beyond acting that one cherishes this vivid, elated little creature – it is for the true star's quality, the quality of being.'

Philip Oakes for the *Sunday Telegraph* wrote this eulogy: 'Always fascinating to watch, she can make much out of little; she is a star; the genuine outsize article, an actress of power and subtlety and a singer whose way with a song is nothing short of marvellous. She is a great artist. She is Judy. She is the very best there is or ever has been.'

On the concert circuit, however, her reviews were now a great deal shakier and usually they would be overtaken by ghoulish news stories about her physical collapse. The last great concert she had given at Carnegie Hall in April 1961 was marred by gossip that she had an iron lung in her dressing-room to solve her breathing problems, and her weight would now career from bloated to emaciated, depending on the number and nature of the pills she was popping. Begelman and Fields had of necessity assigned a young assistant to travel with and babysit Judy full-time and to ensure that she somehow got where she was meant to be and usually but by no means always, on-stage.

Her divorce from Sid Luft had come through in 1962 at Lake Tahoe, and Judy then went back to Las Vegas for one last season. But the Luft relationship was proving as volatile in divorce as it had been in marriage, and Judy now became convinced that her ex-husband was going to kidnap their two children, especially as he filed suit claiming that she was totally unfit to look after them. Unable to get another television series, she contented herself with guest shots on the specials of such old friends from the Rat Pack as Frank Sinatra and Dean Martin, but Judy was now fast running out of theatres or concert halls where managements were prepared any longer to put up with her dressing-room hysterics or, worse, failure to appear at all.

ABOVE *With Dirk Bogarde in* I Could Go On Singing. ☆

As for so many other stars on the way down, Australia seemed to offer a final chance to salvage something from the wreckage of her concert career, but there again she had to face hostile fans already fed up with her late arrivals on stage or her collapse in mid-set. On the way home to California, she collapsed in Hong Kong and there were the usual rumours of yet another attempted suicide. Just before she left Australia, Judy had picked up another young disciple, a gay singer/songwriter called Peter Allen, whom she rapidly passed on to her daughter, Liza, still in her late teens, who married him. Predictably, that marriage lasted about as long as Judy's next.

Back in California, the press coverage showed a new man at her side. This man was a young American actor called Mark Herron, who soon became her fourth husband, albeit very briefly. Judy always attracted fanatical fans, some of whom took on themselves the job of caring for her, a job which eventually always defeated them. At first Mark was just one of the usual hoard of hangers-on, but after he had followed her to Australia and Hong Kong Judy took a particular fancy to him and, as with all her previous relationships, convinced herself that only he could rescue her. But, given that what she was trying to escape from was herself, it was a losing battle from the beginning.

Judy's attempts to marry him had been reduced to the level of farce. On one occasion, coming out

of a coma in Hong Kong, she dragged him to a Norwegian ship in the harbour there, intending to be married by the captain. It then transpired that any marriage on a ship in port is invalid, so they called in a Buddhist priest who made them sign forms in Chinese which neither of them could understand. Subsequently they discovered that all this effort had been in vain since Judy had forgotten to finalize her divorce from Sid Luft.

Judy was now in worse shape than ever, fighting and feuding with Herron almost from the day of their marriage until a weekend six months later when, after a drunken brawl which left them both covered in blood, she set fire to all his clothing. Herron disappeared from her life as quickly and quietly as he had entered it.

By the end of 1964, Judy's bleak situation could be all too easily summarized: no less than eight lawsuits were pending against her, mostly arising from the television series or for the Luft marriage; she was more than half a million dollars in debt, and the IRS now started suing her for unpaid back taxes.

In a curious way, it was this totally catastrophic financial situation which kept her on the road. She now sang in Toronto, Hollywood and Miami, as well as making regular television appearances for Sammy Davis Jr, Perry Como and Ed Sullivan. But the harder she worked, the worse it got. Early in 1966 the bailiffs took over her California home, and her elder sister committed suicide. Wherever

Judy turned, death and taxes were indeed now the only certainties.

For a while Liza and Peter Allen tried to shelter her from the debt-collectors and the angry fans, as yet another concert appearance turned into a fiasco, but even they were finally forced to admit that Judy was way out of control, and the relationship with her elder daughter had not been easy since the two of them appeared in a memorable London Palladium concert a few months earlier at which Judy's little girl suddenly became a fearsome stage rival.

Those of us at that Palladium concert could see this power shift taking place before our eyes and, while it was thrilling to watch, it was clear that Judy had not been prepared for the audience's reaction to Liza. The louder the cheers for Minnelli, the more chilly and beady Judy became, the more fixed the famous smile. That one night turned a daughter into a dangerous challenge and their relationship never completely recovered.

In these last few years of her all too short life, Judy's behaviour pattern became not only predictable but alarmingly repetitive. Eventually, Liza told her mother that she really had to give up on the suicide attempts as nobody, even among her nearest and dearest, could be bothered to pull her out of yet another. Each amazingly disastrous one-night stand would be followed routinely by an amazingly triumphant comeback in the next city and by the end of 1965, plagued by cash and health

RIGHT *The last movie, the last scene: Judy with Dirk Bogarde in* I Could Go On Singing. ☆

BELOW *Judy and Liza together for their only London concert appearance at the London Palladium in July 1964.* ☆

problems, a lifelong addiction to drugs and alcohol began taking their toll. She was simply wearing out, well before she was forty-five.

For a while, London remained her lucky city, and she was even still able to upstage the Beatles there at the 1965 'Night of a Hundred Stars'. But as Liza's career began to take off, Judy's was sinking fast into an abyss from which she no longer had the strength, or the energy, or maybe even the desire to climb out for very long. Like some great battleship firing on its own rescuers, Judy now turned most savagely on those who had tried to love her. During the Herron divorce in 1965 she even announced that, of her recent husbands, 'Minnelli is a very nice man; Luft turned out to be a nice man after all, but Mark Herron only married me for business reasons of his own.'

Since the Luft divorce she and Sid had remained in constant touch, not only because they shared two children, but also because of countless legal tangles, in some of which they were simply suing each other, while in others they were united against some common foe, usually a television or film company for whom Judy had at some point failed to complete a contract. Judy and Sid were much like George and Martha in *Who's Afraid of Virginia Woolf*, locked together by their fights as well as by the memory of a passionately romantic if mutually destructive marriage.

By 1967, Luft was once again managing Garland, who was now reduced to sleeping on the floors of

New York apartments, rented by Liza's friends; there was simply nowhere else she could afford to live. That summer, Luft briefly got her back into good enough shape to return to the Palace Theater, the scene of her first great concert triumph sixteen years earlier. But now, as the *New York Times* noted, the old magic was harder to find. 'Her voice is now tight and husky, but as she goes along she seems to shake it loose by the sheer energy of her singing. She stays safely in a very modest range until she reaches the end of 'Almost Like Being in Love'. Then, she reaches back for one of her old climaxes and just about manages to find it.'

As usual, triumph was immediately followed by disaster. Following the Palace gig, Sid booked her into the Garden State Arts Center in New Jersey, where she set up a new landmark in her own decline by contriving to fall sound asleep on stage in mid-concert as some lethal combination of booze and Benzedrine kicked in.

Now paranoid and on the very edge of real madness, she got engaged to a publicist called Tom Green, whom she then denounced to the police as having stolen all her jewellery. In fact, at her behest, all he had done was take it to the nearest pawnshop so that at least one bill could be settled.

After she had been thrown out of New York's elegant St Mortiz Hotel for non-payment of a $2,000 bed and breakfast bill, she began to haunt a newly fashionable nightclub run by Richard Burton's first wife, Sybil, and it was there, one night in the

RIGHT *Live at London Palladium.* ☆

summer of 1967, that she struck up a friendship with the night manager, a good-looking young man called Mickey Deans. Like Mark Herron, he at first believed that he alone could save Judy from herself and, again like Mark Herron, he was wrong.

Garland now began to give long, rambling interviews to anybody with a tape recorder and some time to spare, vaguely hoping that she might one day be able to turn their tapes into the auto-biography which seemed her only remaining chance of making any money. The problem here was that, by the time she got around to these interviews, usually late at night in some hotel or motel bar, she was invariably so drunk that, in endless monologues, there would only be the occasional moment of truth or, at least, her truth. On one of these tapes she announces, of the only man willing to manage her even after a messy divorce, 'Sid Luft is an animal'; and, on another, she finally admits, 'The trouble with me is that I have never been able to love anyone very much, not even my own children. In the end, I guess I only really love myself and, on a good night, the audience.'

But there remained a widespread belief that Judy could still sell a few tickets and in these last few months of her life it was variously announced that she would lead a take-over or road-show cast of either *Hello, Dolly!* or *Mame*, or, better yet, open the first American production of Lionel Bart's *Maggie May*, a show which was, in the event, never to cross the Atlantic.

LEFT *Judy and Liza backstage at the Palladium.* ☆

She was now using Peter Allen and his brother as a warm-up act and encouraging Liza to stay with him even though she now knew that, like Mark Herron, he had a long history of bisexuality and was openly gay backstage. Allen was ultimately to die of AIDS not long after his divorce from Liza. The IRS, in a final and desperate attempt to obtain at least a few of the thousands of dollars they were owed, were garnishing her concert fees (i.e. they were being paid directly to the tax authorities), thus leaving Judy and her younger children with no income of any kind. She no longer even had a house or jewellery to sell. She was, for all practical purposes, destitute. It was once again Sid Luft who took over the raising of their two children, while Liza temporarily abandoned her concert life to go legit in the first of many musicals written for her by John Kander and Fred Ebb, the off-Broadway *Flora the Red Menace*.

As Judy continued to stagger around the club and concert circuit, one or two perceptive critics began to notice something remarkable about her followers: 'The most fascinating phenomenon,' wrote the *New York Times* in 1964, 'of modern showbusiness is the long and widely publicized love affair between Judy Garland and her followers. They are extremely aware that Garland's voice is now just a memory, that she is often off-pitch, and that she frequently forgets even her most familiar lyrics. But the audience is amazingly quick to respond to the potent fervor that she packs into her delivery, even when her voice quavers and cracks. She also has a wondrous sense of showmanship.'

Towards the end of 1965, she was able to pick up $35,000 for a series of Los Angeles concerts at the Greek Theater, but by now her oldest friends were frequently having to finish these concerts for her. Mickey Rooney, Martha Raye and Johnny Mathis would all take to the spotlight unbilled to try to cover for Judy, who was as often as not now to be found flat out on the floor of her dressing-room. Yet her name still meant something on a poster, and a few weeks after the LA concerts, she appeared at the Houston Astrodome with The Supremes as her supporting act. There, however, only 8,000 people turned out in a sports stadium holding 45,000, and some embarrassing photographs of rows of empty seats did not improve her public image.

The divorce from Mark Herron was also getting her some very messy press coverage. One of her affidavits charged him with physically kicking her

RIGHT *Judy on stage in 1965.* ☆

when she was down. 'If I did kick her,' responded Herron, 'it was purely in self-defence. She can still be a very tough lady.' To another journalist around the same time, Judy spelt out the precise cash crisis she was now facing: 'Once I was worth millions, but today I haven't got a dime. Once I had everybody at my feet, today only the name counts – the money is all gone. Altogether I must have earned around eight million dollars in my life, a million of that before I was eighteen. All I have to show for it is a debt of something like a million; I really don't know where it's all gone.'

Old friends who had been more careful with their money, such as the songwriter Harold Arlen, now began to bankroll her regularly. After one last winter in Las Vegas, where one critic headlined his review 'Will Our Judy Ever Make It Over the Rainbow Again?', she took on one final London contract, this time at the prominent nightclub The Talk of the Town. Once again, this turned into a total fiasco. Several nights during the run she would fail to appear at all, and on other nights she would keep her audience waiting until well past midnight before she could get herself on-stage. One night, an irate fan grabbed her microphone from her and asked, 'If you can't make it on time, why bother to turn up at all?'

The only good thing that happened to Judy during this last London season was that her divorce finally came through and she was therefore able, on 15 March 1969, at the Chelsea Register Office, to

ABOVE *Judy with her fifth and last husband, Mickey Deans, a few months before her death.* ☆

marry her fifth and last husband, Mickey Deans, the man who had been attempting without success to keep her on her feet and reasonably sober for the last nine months.

Judy would now drag him on-stage for her few remaining concerts, the way she had once insisted on having her children join her on the stage and on television to demonstrate a supposedly happy domestic life which was, in fact, then and now, totally mythical. In real life, she was now drinking with virtually anybody who would stay to the end of one of her shows, and thus the gangster Ronnie Kray became an unlikely late-life companion.

As the journalist Sean French later noted, the Garland stage concerts now had a ritual all their own. 'They would begin with rumours of her non-appearance. There would have been a recent suicide attempt, a marriage break-up, or an ignominious public disaster. Finally, the bird-like, appallingly dressed, tousle-headed star would totter on to the stage, professing her nervousness in quavering tones. She would stumble into a song, forgetting the words and having to begin again, after a whispered consultation with her long-suffering conductor. She would then usually fall over while attempting to dance. By now, the audience would be wondering whether they were witnessing the end of Garland's career or maybe even of her life. But then, probably with the yearning tones of 'Over The Rainbow', she would suddenly pull herself together and deliver and hour or two of magnificent performance in a

whole range of styles both comic and tragic… the audience would then go home, purged with the breathless sense of having witnessed genius. Garland would return to her hotel room, to her pills and the vodka, and perhaps another breakdown… No Garland fan could ever complain in subsequent years about sordid revelations tarnishing her legend; that legend was built on them.'

Deans now booked Judy and Johnnie Ray, whose career, built entirely on his dubious ability to cry while singing, was now also in freefall, on what turned out to be her last ever European tour. This collapsed rapidly in Stockholm after one especially terrible night at the end of March, when the audience began to jeer her increasing inability to remember even the lyric of 'Over The Rainbow'. Subsequent bookings in Paris and Rome were, not surprisingly, abruptly cancelled.

Judy and Mickey returned to the mews house they had been lent in London and, on 22 Saturday June, after a blazing row the night before which had ended with Judy screaming at Mickey from outside their front door, Deans awoke to the sound of a ringing telephone. The call was from California for Judy, but the other side of the bed was empty and the door to the bathroom locked. Alarmed, he climbed in through a window, and found Judy sitting on the lavatory, stone cold dead. She was forty-seven years old, $4 million in debt, and, as her old Scarecrow, Ray Bolger, said on American radio that day, 'Judy didn't die, she just plain wore out.'

11. Epilogue

'Accidental death by an incautious dose of barbiturates,' wrote the Chelsea coroner, Gavin Thurston, for the inquest following the inevitable post mortem which is legally mandated whenever the cause of death is in question, 'this is a clear picture of someone who had been habituated to barbiturates in the form of Seconal for a very long period of time, and who on the night of June 22nd/23rd perhaps in a state of confusion from a previous dose (although this is pure speculation) took more barbiturate than her body could tolerate.' The coroner also pointed out, rather touchingly, 'It is important to make public that on this occasion there was no question of alcoholism.'

'The middle of the road was never where Mother was. If she was happy she wasn't just happy, she was ecstatic, and when she was sad, she was sadder than anybody in the whole wide world'

Liza Minnelli

A Harley Street surgeon, Philip Lebon, added, 'Judy had been living on borrowed time. When I first examined her about eight years ago she already had chronic cirrhosis of the liver, and I thought that if she lasted five more years she would have done very well indeed. She lived three years longer than I thought she would; but then she was always a fighter.'

Her old radio partner, Bing Crosby, had once said, 'There isn't a thing that girl cannot do except look after herself,' and if, in the words of one of her most famous songs, Judy was indeed born in a trunk, her tragedy was perhaps that she never really managed to clamber out of it.

After a series of swift, panic telephone calls from Mickey Deans in London to Liza and Peter Allen in New York, as well as Sid and Lorna and Joey Luft in California, it was decided that Judy should have a New York funeral and that, for the first time since the death of Rudolf Valentino in 1921, the coffin would be left open so that her fans could say a last tearful farewell to the singer who more than any other of her generation (with the possible exception of Edith Piaf in France) had plugged herself directly into the hearts if not the minds of her followers.

21,000 of them queued to pay their last respects at Campbell's Funeral Home and, at the funeral which followed two days later, it was James Mason, her husband in *A Star is Born*, who gave the final address: 'You close your eyes and you see a small, vivid woman, sometimes fat, sometimes thin, but vivid and vital … I travelled in her orbit for only a while, but it was an exciting while, and one during which it seemed that the joys in her life outbalanced all the miseries. The little girl whom I knew when she was good, was not only very, very good, but also the most sympathetic, the funniest, the sharpest and the most stimulating woman I ever knew. She gave so much and so richly that there was no currency in which to repay her, and she needed to be repaid, needed devotion and love beyond the resources of any of us. Judy's gift was to wring tears from men with hearts of rock.'

Later that day, Liza gave a more intimate memoir to the magazine *Rolling Stone*, 'When we travelled with Mamma, we always travelled with charisma … there were never less than twenty-six pieces of luggage, and I'm talking checkable luggage. The hand stuff, forget it: shopping bags, food bags, medicine bags. I was always in charge of her personal ice bucket which she just had to have. It was her firm belief that there would never be anything, ever, in any hotel in the world that she could just order from room service. But I never minded, because Mother almost always made it such fun. She was truly one of the funniest people I have ever known. Often we had to sneak out of hotels down the service elevator in the middle of the night because she couldn't pay the bill, but she would make a game even out of that. We would put on all the clothes we could, about five layers, and then just walk out leaving the rest. Mamma would say, "Hell, I needed a new wardrobe anyway."'

Among those who attended the funeral were such old friends and colleagues as Mickey Rooney, Ray Bolger, Lauren Bacall, Katharine Hepburn, Lana Turner, June Allyson and Jack Benny, who noted that this was the only show for which Judy had actually turned up on time.

Frank Sinatra paid all her funeral expenses and noted presciently, 'Judy will now have a kind of mystic survival. She was the greatest. All the rest of us will be forgotten soon after we die, but never Judy.'

Indeed, it could be argued, as Gore Vidal did of Truman Capote, that death was Garland's wisest career move. The legend which had started to take hold even before her death soon became rooted in the memory of audiences all over the world, while even those who had never seen her live in concert fell in love with her Dorothy as *The Wizard of Oz* became, throughout the 1970s and 80s, the movie most often shown on television.

But there was also the Garland curse – both her daughters, Liza and Lorna, were to follow her into the business, but both have also suffered at least temporarily from the drink and drug problems which had always haunted their mother. Happily, in their generation, clinics had sprung up all over the world far better able to deal with these personal addictions than the drug-dispensing hospitals of Judy's time. There is also no longer anything like the same public opprobrium attached to their problems as there was for Judy.

They have both had a rocky matrimonial past and, as of this writing, Liza particularly has not been able to find a partner who can cope over the long haul with that curiously Garlandesque combination of insecurity and starriness. Their mother's propensity for stagefright and panic before a concert has been passed on to both girls, and they have each had to deal with it with varying degrees of success.

As Lorna has written in her memoirs, 'All three of us Judy children developed serious addiction problems. In spite of what we experienced as children, or more accurately because of it, we each followed a similar path. For me and Liza, it was cocaine and alcohol and, in Liza's case, pills as well. For Joey, it was primarily alcohol … Unfortunately, addiction wasn't the only destructive pattern that ran in the family; we also found it amazingly difficult to choose the right partners.'

Both girls have had many years of professional help and both attract the same kind of fanatical, often gay, fans. Even their mother's inability to control her weight seems to be genetic – a photograph of Liza at Frank Sinatra's funeral in 1998 showed a bloated, puffy face above a hugely inflated body. Not a year earlier, the svelte, almost emaciated Liza had given a series of sold-out, triumphant concerts at Radio City Music Hall in New York, where Liza, like her mother, was for a while easily able to fill the 5,000-plus seats with roaring applause.

ABOVE *Dorothy lives: the 1991 official US Post Office stamp.* ☆

Echoes of Garland's brief career trajectory can be found in the lives of Edith Piaf, Marlene Dietrich, Elizabeth Taylor and, perhaps most directly, the Marilyn Monroe who once followed Judy around a Hollywood party saying, 'Don't get too far away from me, I'm really scared,' to which Garland replied, 'Honey, we are all scared all the time. Being scared is what we do best.'

Some years after Judy's death, reviewing one of the twenty or more biographies which have become a cottage industry, it was the ballerina Moira Shearer who most succinctly made the case against Garland in later life: 'Her last two husbands do not even bear thinking about, but by then she was wrecked by drugged, drunken self-indulgence. Up to her ears in debt, she was still trying to perform in the only nightspots that would employ her ... she had immense theatrical talent allied to a marvellous voice, but both were ruined by arrogance and uncontrolled hysteria ... she was also an inveterate liar, vengeful, jealous of colleagues and especially her daughter Liza, always meanest to those who had made her career possible. Her treatment of her mother was abominable.'

Having been trapped at MGM for years as a teenager, age eventually caught up with Judy so fast that when she died in her mid-forties she already seemed much older. Her final concerts were not so much entertainments as ambulance-chases, but there was still always the memory of Dorothy. If this film was a farewell to innocence, it was America's as well as Dorothy's, and by the time that 'Over the Rainbow' had become everything from an AIDS requiem to an anthem of sexual freedom, it was clear that we were in darker territory than even the Wicked Witch of the West could ever have envisaged.

Looking more closely today at what lay beyond the rainbow, it is possible to see that Judy's paradise had been lost for some time: 'Toto, I have a feeling we're not in Kansas any more.' The garish, candy colours of Oz can now be seen as a forerunner of everything that was to become most objectionable in a Disneyland universe.

In her later performances, Judy had taken more and more often to singing a lyric of Noël Coward's from *Bitter Sweet* which ran, 'For I believe that since my life began, the most I've had is just a talent to amuse.' That could be one of her epitaphs, but there is perhaps a better one in something the Wizard of Oz says to the Tin Man at the end of the picture: 'Remember, a heart is not judged by how much you love, but how much you are loved by others.' Poor Judy. By her own admission she loved nobody but herself, and when she ceased even to like herself very much, it was hardly surprising that she neither loved much nor was loved much in return, except by strangers.

Perhaps the final irony of Garland's life is that the woman idolized as a great survivor in fact failed to survive at all. Most of her songs were not reflections but denials of her own life. Judy almost

LEFT *A rare picture of Judy with all her children – Liza Minnelli, Lorna Luft and little Joey Luft.* ☆

never had herself a Merry Little Christmas, no matter how often she sang about it, nor did the man on the trolley ride with her to the end of the line, and if when her name is mentioned, one immediately recalls any single moment from her movies, it is surely that little girl in Kansas asking, plaintively, 'Why, oh why, can't I?'

In the end, the miracle of Judy Garland is the way in which thirty years after her death, her movies and recordings are showing and selling as never before. No week on television anywhere in the world is complete without one of her films, and in New York in 1999, one of the all-time best sellers is a boxed set of her videos and CDs, going for more than $100 a time.

If this celebration has seemed unduly focused on the chaos of her life as distinct from the glory of much of her career, it is also worth remembering that no singer, with the possible exception of Frank Sinatra has become so identified with the American century or so immediately evocative of its music. The tragedy of AIDS, coming as it did years after her death, only served to heighten the already existing impression that Judy's was the voice of a tormented and traumatised minority, as well as of the romantic dreams of more mainstream audience.

The key to her now-legendary status is that you can find in Judy's songs the affirmation of almost anything you happen to be looking for at the time; and one look at that strangely tortured child star, growing almost overnight into the woman carrying the weight of the world on her fragile shoulders, is also a guarantee of instant heartbreak. If we all love Judy, and most of us surely do, it is in the end because she represents the best and worst of all her audiences. Judy is what we hoped the world would be like, and Garland is what we feared it would soon become; that is why she will live forever in all of our dreams and only some of our worst nightmares.

Filmography

PIGSKIN PARADE 20TH CENTURY FOX, 1936
Producer: Darryl F. Zanuck
Director: David Butler
Cast: Stuart Erwin, Patsy Kelly, Jack Haley, John Downs, Betty Grable, Arline Judge, Dixie Dunbar, Judy Garland, Anthony Martin, Fred Kohler, Jr. Elisha Cook, Jr. Julius Tannen, Si Jenks

BROADWAY MELODY OF 1938 MGM, 1937
Producer: Jack Cummings
Director: Roy Del Ruth
Cast: Robert Taylor, Eleanor Powell, George Murphy, Binnie Barnes, Buddy Ebsen, Sophie Tucker, Judy Garland, Charles Igor Gorin, Raymond Walburn, Robert Benchley, Willie Howard, Charley Grapewin, Robert Wildhack, Billy Gilbert, Barnett Parker, Helen Troy

THOROUGHBREDS DON'T CRY MGM, 1937
Producer: Harry Rapf
Director: Alfred E. Green
Cast: Judy Garland, Mickey Rooney, Sophie Tucker, C. Aubrey Smith, Ronald Sinclair, Forrester Harvey, Charles D. Brown, Frankie Darro, Henry Kolker, Helen Troy

EVERYBODY SING MGM, 1938
Producer: Harry Rapf
Director: Edwin L. Marin
Cast: Allan Jones, Judy Garland, Fanny Brice, Reginald Owen, Billie Burke, Reginald Gardiner, Lynne Carver, Helen Troy, Monty Woolley, Adia Kuznetzoff, Henry Armetta, Michellette Burani, Mary Forbes

LISTEN, DARLING MGM, 1938
Producer: Jack Cummings, *Director*: Edwin L. Marin
Cast: Freddie Bartholomew, Judy Garland, Mary Astor, Walter Pidgeon, Alan Hale, Scotty Beckett, Barnett Parker, Gene Lockhart, Charley Grapewin

LOVE FINDS ANDY HARDY MGM, 1938
Producer: Carey Wilson (uncredited)
Director: George B. Seitz
Cast: Lewis Stone, Mickey Rooney, Cecilia Parker, Fay Holden, Judy Garland, Lana Turner, Ann Rutherford, Mary Howard, Gene Reynolds, Don Castle, Betty Ross Clarke, Marie Blake, George Breakston, Raymond Hatton, Frank Darien

THE WIZARD OF OZ MGM, 1939
Producer: Mervyn LeRoy
Director: Victor Fleming
Cast: Judy Garland, Frank Morgan, Ray Bolger, Bert Lahr, Jack Haley, Margaret Hamilton, Billie Burke, Charley Grapewin, Clara Blandick, Pat Walshe, The Singer Midgets

BABES IN ARMS MGM, 1939
Producer: Arthur Freed
Director: Busby Berkeley
Cast: Mickey Rooney, Judy Garland, Charles Winninger, Guy Kibbee, June Preisser, Grace Hayes, Betty Jaynes, Douglas McPhail, Rand Brooks, Leni Lynnsw, John Sheffield, Henry Hull, Barnett Parker, Ann Shoemaker, Margaret Hamilton, Joseph Crehan, George McKay, Henry Roquemore, Lelah Tyler, Lon McCallister, Sidney Miller

ANDY HARDY MEETS DEBUTANTE MGM, 1940
Producer: Carey Wilson (uncredited)
Director: George B. Seitz
Cast: Lewis Stone, Mickey Rooney, Cecilia Parker, Fay Holden, Judy Garland, Ann Rutherford, Diana Lewis, George Breakston, Sara Haden, Addison Richards, George Lessey, Cy Kendall, Clyde Willson, Charles Coleman

STRIKE UP THE BAND MGM, 1940
Producer: Arthur Freed
Director: Busby Berkeley
Cast: Mickey Rooney, Judy Garland, Paul Whiteman, June Preisser, William Tracy, Larry Nunn, Margaret Early, Ann Shoemaker, Francis Pierlot, Virginia Brissac, George Lessey, Enid Bennett, Howard Hickman, Sarah Edwards, Milton Kibbee, Helen Jerome Eddy, Joe Yule, Gene Kelly

LITTLE NELLIE KELLY MGM, 1940
Producer: Arthur Freed
Director: Norman Taurog
Cast: Judy Garland, George Murphy, Charles Winninger, Douglas McPhail, Arthur Shields, Rita Page, Forrester Harvey, James Burke, George Watts

ZIEGFELD GIRL MGM, 1941
Producer: Pandro S. Berman
Director: Robert Z. Leonard
Cast: James Stewart, Judy Garland, Hedy Lamarr, Lana Turner, Tony Martin, Jackie Cooper, Ian Hunter, Charles Winninger, Edward Everett Horton, Philip Dorn, Paul Kelly, Eve Arden, Dan Dailey, Al Shean, Fay Holden, Felix Bressart, Rose Hobart, Bernard Nedell, Ed McNamara, Mae Busch, Renie Riano, Josephine Whittell

LIFE BEGINS FOR ANDY HARDY MGM, 1941
Producer: Carey Wilson (uncredited)
Director: George B. Seitz
Cast: Lewis Stone, Mickey Rooney, Judy Garland, Fay Holden, Ann Rutherford, Sara Haden, Patricia Dane, Ray McDonald, George Breakston, Pierre Watkin

BABES ON BROADWAY MGM, 1941
Producer: Arthur Freed
Director: Busby Berkeley
Starring: Mickey Rooney, Judy Garland, Fay Bainter, Virginia Weidler, Ray McDonald, Richard Quine, Donald Meek, Alexander Woollcott, Luis Alberni, James Gleason, Emma Dunn, Frederick Burton, Cliff Clark, William Post, Jr., Donna Reed, Joe Yule, Margaret O'Brien, Carl Stockdale, Dick Baron, Will Lee, Stop, Look and Listen Trio, Tom Hanlon, Renee Austin, Roger Steele, Bryant Washburn, Charles Wagenheim, Arthur Hoyt, Jack Lipson, Dorothy Morris, Maxine Flores, Sidney Miller, King Baggott, Barbara Bedford, Shimen Ruskin, Jean Porter, Leslie Brooks, Roger Moore, Ava Gardner

FOR ME AND MY GAL MGM, 1942
Producer: Arthur Freed
Director: Busby Berkeley
Cast: Judy Garland, George Murphy, Gene Kelly, Marta Eggerth, Ben Blue, Richard Quine, Horace (Stephen) McNally, Lucille Norman, Keenan Wynn

PRESENTING LILY MARS MGM, 1943
Producer: Joe Pasternak
Director: Norman Taurog
Cast: Judy Garland, Van Heflin, Fay Bainter, Richard Carlson, Spring Byrington, Marta Eggerth, Connie Gilchrist, Leonid Kinskey, Patricia Barker, Janet Chapman, Annabelle Logan, Douglas Croft, Ray McDonald

GIRL CRAZY MGM, 1943

Producer: Arthur Freed
Director: Norman Taurog
Cast: Mickey Rooney, Judy Garland, Gil Stratton, Robert E. Strictland, Rags Ragland, June Allyson, Nancy Walker, Guy Kibbee, Frances Rafferty, Howard Freeman, Henry O' Neill

MEET ME IN ST LOUIS MGM, 1944

Producer: Arthur Freed
Director: Vincente Minnelli
Cast: Judy Garland, Margaret O'Brien, Mary Astor, Lucille Bremer, Tom Drake, Marjorie Main, Leon Ames, Harry Davenport, June Lockhart, Henry Daniels Jr, Joan Carroll, Hugh Marlowe, Robert Sully, Chill Wills

THE CLOCK MGM, 1945

Producer: Arthur Freed
Director: Vincente Minnelli
Cast: Judy Garland, Robert Walker, James Gleason, Keenan Wynn, Mashall Thompson, Lucille Gleason, Ruth Brady, Moyna Macgill

THE HARVEY GIRLS MGM,1946

Producer: Arthur Freed
Director: George Sidney
Cast: Judy Garland, John Hodiak, Ray Bolger, Angela Lansbury, Preston Foster, Virginia O'Brien, Kenny Baker, Majorie Main, Chill Wills, Selena Royle, Cyd Charisse, Ruth Brady

ZIEGFELD FOLLIES OF 1946 MGM, 1946

Producer: Arthur Freed
Director: Vincente Minnelli
Cast: Edward Arnold, Fred Astaire, Lucille Ball, Marion Bell, Lucille Bremer, Fanny Brice, Bunin's Puppets, Cyd Charisse, Hume Cronyn, William Frawley, Judy Garland, Kathryn Grayson, Lena Horne, Gene Kelly, Robert Lewis, James Melton, Victor Moore, Virginia O'Brien, William Powell, Red Skelton, Esther Williams, Keenan Wynn

TILL THE CLOUDS ROLL BY MGM, 1946

Producer: Arthur Freed
Director: Richard Whorf
Cast: Robert Walker, Judy Garland, Lucille Bremer, Van Heflin, Paul Langton, Dorothy Patrick, Mary Nash, Van Johnson, Dinah Shore, Harry Hayden, Paul Macey, Joan Wells

THE PIRATE MGM, 1948

Producer: Arthur Freed
Director: Vincente Minnelli
Cast: Judy Garland, Gene Kelly, Walter Slezak, Gladys Cooper, Reginald Owen, George Zucco, The Nicholas Brothers, Lester Allen, Lola Deem, Ellen Ross, Mary Jo Ellis, Jean Dean

EASTER PARADE MGM, 1948

Producer: Arthur Freed
Director: Charles Walters
Cast: Judy Garland, Fred Astaire, Peter Lawford, Ann Miller, Jules Munshin, Clinton Sundberg, Jeni Le Gon

IN THE GOOD OLD SUMMERTIME MGM, 1949

Producer: Joe Pasternak
Director: Robert E Leonard
Cast:Judy Garland, Van Johnson, S.Z. ("Cuddles") Sakall, Spring Byrington, Buster Keaton, Marcia Van Dyke, Clinton Sundberg, Lillian Bronson, Ralph Sanford

SUMMER STOCK MGM, 1950

Producer: Joe Pasternak
Director: Charles Walters
Cast: Judy Garland, Gene Kelly, Eddie Bracken, Gloria DeHaven, Marjorie Main, Phil Silvers, Ray Collins, Nita Bieber, Carleton Carpenter, Hans Conried

A STAR IS BORN WARNER BROS, 1954

Producer: Sidney Luft
Director: George Cukor
Cast: Judy Garland, James Mason, Jack Carson, Charles Bickford, Tom Noonan

PEPE COLUMBIA PICTURES, 1960

Produced & Directed by George Sidney
Cast: Cantinflas, Judy Garland, Shirley Jones, Dan Dailey, Carlos Montalban, Edward G. Robinson, William Demarest, Ernie Kovacs, Matt Mattox, Vicki Trickett, Hank Henry

JUDGEMENT AT NUREMBERG UA, 1961

Produced & Direced by Stanley Kramer
Cast: Spencer Tracy, Burt Lancaster, Richard Widmark, Marlene Dietrich, Maximilian Schell, Judy Garland, Montgomery Clift, William Shatner, Edward Binns, Kenneth MacKenna, Werner Klemperer, Alan Baxter, Torben Meyer

A CHILD IS WAITING UA, 1963

Producer: Stanley Kramer
Director: Philip Langner
Cast: Burt Lancaster, Judy Garland, Gena Rowlands, Steven Hill, Bruce Ritchey, Gloria McGehee, Paul Stewart, Lawrence Tierney, Elizabeth Wilson, Barbara Pepper, John Morley, Marlo Gallo, Fredrick Draper

I COULD GO ON SINGING UA, 1963

Producers: Stuart Millar & Lawrence Turman
Director: Ronald Neame
Cast: Judy Garland, Dirk Bogarde, Jack Klugman, Gregory Phillips, Aline MacMahon, Pauline Jameson, Jeremy Burnham

Acknowledgements

Every reasonable effort has been made to acknowledge the ownership of copyrighted photographs included in this volume. Any errors that have inadvertently occurred will be corrected in subsequent editions provided notification is sent to the publisher.

Alpha
10, 44, 90

Aquarius Library
2, 12, 13, 14, 17, 18, 20, 30, 35, 37, 40, 42, 46, 50, 53, 58, 59, 60, 63, 64, 66, 69, 71, 75, 78, 82, 88, 91, 94, 96, 98, 101, 103, 109, 116, 117, 119, 120, 122, 124, 126, 127, 129, 131, 141, 143 (top), 146, 148, 150, 151, 152, 153, 154, 155, 159

Kobal Collection
7, 15, 19, 23, 24, 25, 26, 27, 28, 31, 32, 39, 49, 51, 52, 55, 57, 61, 67, 70, 73, 74, 76, 81, 84, 87, 89, 90, 91, 92, 93, 94, 95, 97, 104, 107, 108, 110, 111, 112, 115, 128, 133, 137, 139, 140, 143 (bottom), 145, 149, 158,

Redferns © B. Willoughby
9, 95, 135, 142, 147, 153

Index

Note: Page numbers in *italics* refer to illustrations.